THE
LONDON
CABBIE'S
QUIZ BOOK

First published in 2020 by White Lion Publishing, an imprint of The Quarto Group.
The Old Brewery, 6 Blundell Street,
London, N7 9BH,
United Kingdom
T (0)20 7700 6700
www.QuartoKnows.com

Text © 2020 Ian Beetlestone

Maps reproduced by permission of Geographers' A-Z Map Co. Ltd. License No. B8525 © Crown Copyright 2020. All rights reserved. License number 100017302

A catalogue record for this book is available from the British Library.

ISBN 978 0 71125 105 2
Ebook ISBN 978 0 71125 106 9

10 9 8 7 6 5 4 3 2 1

Designer: Dave Jones

Printed in China

THE
LONDON CABBIE'S
QUIZ BOOK

Pit your wits against the world's smartest taxi drivers

IAN BEETLESTONE

WHITE LION
PUBLISHING

➡ Contents

One Knowledge examiner, who
was something of an eccentric, was said
to have asked a Knowledge girl to tell him where
the Ring public house was. 'I don't know, sir,' she said.
'Come on,' he said, 'are you sure? Have a think.' 'It's really
familiar, sir, and I'm sure I do know it but I just can't place it,'
came the reply. 'I tell you what,' said the examiner,
'I need a new pen, come with me.'

After leading the baffled Knowledge girl out of the examination room,
down a corridor, through another door, across the staff office and to
a stationery cupboard, through which he proceeded to rummage,
he looked out of the window, pointed across the street and said,
'Oh look – what's that down there?' The student followed his
gaze and replied, 'That's the Ring public house, sir.'

'So it is,' said the examiner, and led her back to
the examination room to continue
her successful appearance.

Regulations require the London
taxi's famous turning circle
to be under 7.6 m (25 ft) to
enable quick manoeuvring in the city's
ancient narrow streets, as well as to navigate
the tight roundabout in the forecourt of the
Savoy Hotel.

The A12 corridor,
leading out into the Essex
suburbs, has long been known
as Green Badge Valley for the
large number of London
cabbies residing there.

Introduction

. . . .

'Has anybody in here got a degree?' demanded the examiner as he opened his introductory talk on the Knowledge of London at the old Public Carriage Office in October 2008. One or two of us in the room sheepishly raised our hands. 'Well, this is harder,' he boomed in his stern cockney accent: 'I used to be in the SAS. I carried eighty kilograms over Dartmoor and let me tell you – this is the hardest thing I've ever done.'

Welcome to a London quiz book like no other. Written by a licensed London taxi driver, *The London Cabbie's Quiz Book* gives readers a chance to test their knowledge of the world's greatest metropolis against the famed London cabbie's intricate and world-beating Knowledge.

The examiner wasn't wrong. The Knowledge – the famously thorough course of study and examinations undertaken by all trainee London cabbies – took me longer to complete than my degree and involved far less fun and many more hours of sheer, hard graft. I got my green badge – the All London taxi driver's licence – in November 2012, after more than four years of intensive study on top of a full-time job. I spent countless hours riding around London on a moped learning 320 set routes around a 9-km (6-mile) radius of Charing Cross, and along the way noted and memorised the locations of thousands of points of interest ('points' for short) – anything from a nondescript Balham boozer to Buckingham Palace. I spent countless hours sweating over laminated maps with my fellow Knowledge students (Knowledge boys and girls, as we call them), reciting routes from one point to another, which my partner traced with a whiteboard pen so we could dissect and perfect them.

When you think you're ready, after a short written test to make sure you can read a map, you begin what are known as 'appearances', which make up the bulk of the Knowledge exams. These are legendarily and inexplicably terrifying. It's just you and the examiner, sitting across a table from one another, dressed in suits and calling each other 'sir' (or, occasionally, 'ma'am'). It's been called 'the last bastion of the empire' for its archaic, regimented formality.

The examiner names a point, and – assuming you know – you tell them where it is. Then they give you another. With their locations satisfactorily established, the examiner says, 'off you go then', and you recite the most direct driving route between the two. After four questions, the examiner tells you whether you did well enough to score points and tells you to come back after fifty-six days' more study for your next appearance.

That's just the first stage, which we call '56s', after the gap between appearances. When you've had enough appearances and scored enough points to get through 56s, the examiner starts telling you to come back in twenty-eight days, and the questions get harder. When you've scored enough points on 28s he tells you to come back in twenty-one days and the questions get harder still. Eventually, when you complete 21s, you are deemed to have achieved the required level of Knowledge (you get your 'req', as we know it in the trade).

Next it's time to learn the suburbs. This is something of a coda to the main body of the Knowledge and merely involves learning scores of set routes from the edges of the 9-km (6-mile) radius out to the suburban districts. For these there's just one appearance, in which you recite a handful of the routes word for word. Nothing to it!

Finally, a few weeks after that, you put on your best clothes and return with your loved ones for a pep talk on life out there in the real world, driving an actual London taxi, and you're called up one by one for a handshake and to be presented with your licence. That's probably the only part that's as easy as doing a degree.

Using this book

This book aims to replicate the Knowledge experience for the reader – consider yourself an armchair Knowledge boy or girl – except hopefully with rather more fun and a little less graft.

Take this, now, as your introductory talk, after which five sets of quizzes follow. First, the map test to get you in the mood. Then three sections of quizzes relating to the area within a 9-km (6-mile) radius of Charing Cross – 56s, 28s and 21s – followed by a further section taking you out into the suburbs. In between it all, I've thrown in a few nuggets of taxi trivia and insider snippets from the trade for your entertainment.

Apart from the map test (which involves no route), all the quizzes in this book are based on actual set routes from the Knowledge itself, beginning with the first route we all learn – Manor House Station to Gibson Square – and ending with the last – Copenhagen Street to Charing Cross Station. In between, I've chosen routes to give the widest possible coverage of the city and tried to make sure I've captured as many of the big sights that one feels ought to be included. The suburban routes, likewise, I have whittled down to nine, chosen for the sights they take in and the widest possible coverage.

As in the real Knowledge, the questions get harder as you progress. But also – like the real Knowledge – you are at the whim of your examiner. If you get a nice examiner on a good day, you might be asked something surprisingly easy. Conversely, if you get a nasty examiner on a bad day, you might get thrown a real stinker. Hence I hope there will be something in most sections for those with only a passing familiarity with London, and equally something to challenge even the meanest Public Carriage Office examiner in the filthiest of moods.

Modern technology has brought new slang into the trade, such as 'pob' – meaning passenger – from the 'person on board' status that was a feature of one of the early 'e-hailing' apps that many drivers now use.

The period around ten o'clock at night is known in the trade as 'burst time' because this is when the myriad double doors of theatres and concert venues are slung open from the inside and all the people who disappeared behind them at around seven-thirty suddenly flow en masse into the streets – and ideally onto the back seats of every passing black cab available.

One of the oddest and most obscure points of interest asked by Knowledge examiners concerns 'the small statue of mice eating cheese'. This is found in the cornicing high on a building in Philpot Lane in the City and is said (possibly apocryphally) to commemorate two workmen who fell from the building during its construction following an argument over stolen sandwiches. It later turned out that mice had been the real culprits.

All questions relate to the route shown on the accompanying map, which is also written out for you at the start of the quiz. This is just how a Knowledge boy or girl would recite the route in an appearance, replete with the parlance of the trade ('comply', for example, saves us the trouble of describing the circle at a roundabout and counting the number of exits). Some of the questions are straightforward general knowledge, but clues for many others may be found on the map or in the route, so if you're stuck, it's possible it might not be quite as hard as it appears. On the other hand, it might just be a stinker.

Many of the routes I have chosen are the most direct ones available between the start and end points, however the more eagle-eyed reader may spot one or two that might not have scored full marks in an actual Knowledge appearance: I have allowed myself a little leeway if going a slightly different way enabled me to capture more interesting topics for questions. I have taken us through the Bank Junction, for example, which was possible when I studied the Knowledge, but is now restricted to buses and bicycles during the daytime. It is extremely rare, after all, to score full marks on every single appearance, and besides, I wouldn't want to be giving away all our cut-throughs. Extra kudos for anyone who can spot where a route could be improved! Any mistakes beyond that I will leave to my colleagues to point out when they see me on the street. . .

Finally, Knowledge of London examiners are renowned for their quirks, and the questions and points asked by each carry the hallmarks of their distinct personalities, which Knowledge boys and girls get to know as they progress. So I make no apology for asking questions about the things that interest me, and hope that you, too, may find as you move through the book that you have got to know your examiner and understand a little of what makes him tick.

Which just about brings your introductory talk to a close – by now you should understand how the book works and what's in store, so you should be ready to turn the page and get on with your first quiz. And as we say in the trade – be lucky!

Map Test

1   What is the name of the complex of concert halls, art galleries and offices in King's Cross that pioneered the redevelopment of the area when it opened in 2008? Which newspaper is based here? Which artist played one of his final London shows here during a series of surprise gigs in February 2014?

2   Which building, opened in 1998, stands on the site of the old St Pancras goods depot? Which neighbouring building houses Europe's biggest biomedical research facility?

3   Which university opened a campus, in which new square in King's Cross, in 2011? What was the building's original purpose?

4   King's Cross is also home to apartments and a park built within what ex-industrial structures?

5   In the nineteenth century, an as yet unpublished author working for a railway company salvaged headstones from a churchyard that was partly in the path of a new line and had them arranged around a tree, where they remain to this day. The tree, which has movingly grown up around the stones, is known by what name (after the author)? Which railway station does the line service? And what is the name of the church?

6   Which Fitzrovia street is home to a private revolving restaurant with spectacular views of the West End?

7   Who founded the foundling hospital in Bloomsbury in 1739? Which square and street nearby are renowned for their specialist hospitals?

8   In which street will you find a museum, art gallery and library that 'aims to challenge how we all think and feel about health'?

9   Which building is the headquarters of a religious organisation founded in England in the seventeenth century? Which street nearby is home to an organisation whose Latin motto translates as 'not apt to disclose secrets'?

10   Which street would you go to if you wanted to see dodo bones?

Stage 1:

The
56s

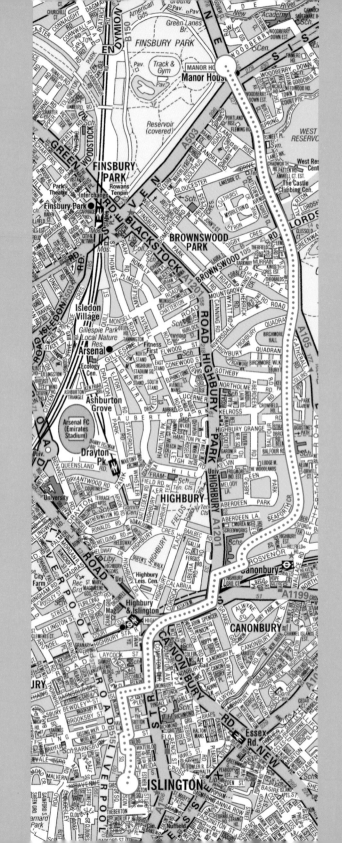

01

Manor House Station, N4 to Gibson Square, N1

Leave on the left Green Lanes, right and right Highbury New Park, left Highbury Grove, right St Paul's Road, comply Highbury Corner, leave by Upper Street, right Islington Park Street, left College Cross, right Barnsbury Street, left Milner Square, forward Milner Place, forward into Gibson Square

1 What was the Manor House that gave its name to the area in which this route starts? What connection do musicians Jimi Hendrix, Jeff Beck and Rod Stewart have with it?

2 Woodberry Wetlands, to the left of Green Lanes shortly after you set off, occupy what, originally built in 1833 to store drinking water from the New River canal? Stone from which (also watery) London landmark, under demolition at the time, was used in the construction of the banks? What activity centre is housed in a decorative Victorian pumping station just south of here?

3 In Highbury Grove, just north of the junction with Highbury New Park, a blue plaque marks the one-time home of Charles Alfred Cruft. What is his legacy?

4 Sixteenth-century Canonbury Tower, just south of St Paul's Road, lays claim to what distinction among Islington's buildings? Perhaps the building's most famous resident, which philosopher and scientist made the tower his home in 1616?

5 A joint first-ever event in the United Kingdom took place at Islington Town Hall on 29th March 2014. What was it?

6 Which two politicians had a much analysed dinner at Granita restaurant (now closed) in Upper Street in 1994?

7 After whom is Islington's Liverpool Road named?

8 Which playwright was briefly imprisoned in the 1960s for defacing books he'd borrowed from Islington Central Library? What street is the library on?

9 Cunningly disguised as a miniature classical temple in response to early nimbyism from residents, a ventilation shaft for which London Underground line can be seen in Gibson Square?

10 Where on this route can you play tennis and bowls?

Taxi joke:
A woman hails a cab
and says to the driver,
'Waterloo'. Driver: 'The
station?' Woman: 'Well,
I'm a bit late for the
battle, love.'

In a courteous
gesture of benefaction,
examiners often ask Manor
House Station to Gibson Square
– the very first route Knowledge
boys and girls learn – as the very
last question on a candidate's
final appearance.

The Knowledge of London was originally
administered by the Metropolitan Police
in New Scotland Yard. From 1919 the
department was housed at police offices
in Lambeth before getting dedicated premises
in Islington in 1966. There it stayed until 2010
when, having been transferred in 2000 to
Transport for London, it moved to Southwark.

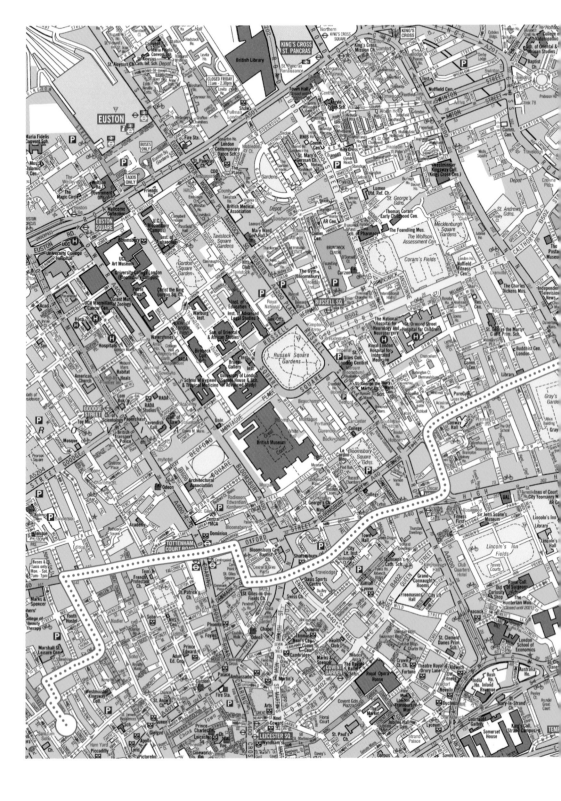

02

Myddelton Square, EC1 to Golden Square, W1

Leave by River Street, left Amwell Street, right Rosebery Avenue, right Clerkenwell Road, forward Theobalds Road, left Drake Street, forward Red Lion Square, forward Procter Street, right High Holborn, forward Princes Circus, forward St Giles High Street, right Earnshaw Street, left New Oxford Street, forward Oxford Street, left Berwick Street, right Broadwick Street, left Marshall Street, right Beak Street, left Upper James Street, forward into Golden Square

1   After which nearby unusual river is River Street named? Why is it unusual, and how is the Myddelton after whom Myddelton Square is named connected with it?

2   Near the end of this river, in the late seventeenth century, Richard Sadler opened what, on the site of what? The site has been used for more-or-less the same purpose ever since. What is its current name?

3   Where in Rosebery Avenue can you ride the old underground Mail Rail, recently restored and opened to the public as an attraction?

4   Rosebery Avenue is named after Archibald Primrose, fifth Earl of Rosebery. What was his greatest claim to fame?

5   Which iconic brutalist building do you pass as you approach Oxford Street? After its completion in 1966 it stood empty for some years. In protest, a charity founded in 1969 took the same name. What was the charity's focus?

6   You enter which district by Berwick Street, home, since the 1840s, to one of the West End's most popular what?

7   In the second half of the twentieth century, Berwick Street also became famous for its record shops. It's fitting, then, that a photograph of the street appeared on the cover of a 1995 album by which zeitgeisty British band? What was the name of the album?

8 On the corner of Broadwick
Street and Lexington Street
you pass a pub named
after the nineteenth-century
physician John Snow. He's also
commemorated by a nearby water pump,
owing to his 1854 discovery that contaminated water was the source of an
outbreak of what disease?

9 A blue plaque marks the spot where, in a house on the corner of
Broadwick Street and Marshall Street, a famous local was born in 1757.
A visionary poet, painter and engraver, his poem 'London' contains the
famous lines, 'I wander thro' each charter'd street, / Near where the
charter'd Thames does flow. / And mark in every face I meet / Marks of
weakness, marks of woe.' What is his name?

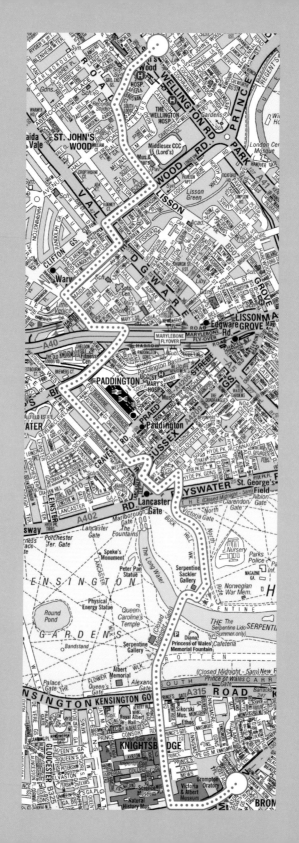

03

St John's Wood Station, NW8 to Brompton Oratory, SW7

Leave on the right Acacia Road, forward and left Grove End Road, right St John's Wood Road, left Maida Vale, right Blomfield Road, left Warwick Avenue, comply Harrow Road Circus, leave by Harrow Road, comply Bishop's Bridge roundabout, leave by Bishop's Bridge Road, left Westbourne Terrace, left and right Sussex Gardens, left Stanhope Terrace, right Brook Street, forward Brook Gate, forward West Carriage Drive, forward Serpentine Road, forward Serpentine Bridge, forward West Carriage Drive, forward Alexandra Gate, forward Exhibition Road, left Cromwell Gardens, forward Thurloe Place, forward Brompton Road, set down on the left

1   Which unusual sculptor lived at 24 Wellington Road, just south of St John's Wood Station, in the late 1830s? The gallery she founded is still open today, on the other side of Regent's Park in Marylebone Road.

2 As you follow the left bend in Grove End Road, why are tourists photographing each other crossing the road just to your right? And which grove is Grove End Road the end of?

3 Just down Harrow Road to the east of Harrow Road Circus is Paddington Green. How, due to the launch of the first regular what in 1829, is it connected with the Bank of England?

4 What's the watery connection between Westbourne Terrace, the Serpentine lake in Hyde Park, Sloane Square Station and the River Thames at Chelsea?

5 Across the Long Water from Serpentine Bridge is a statue to which fictional children's hero? Who had it erected?

6 Brompton Oratory was founded by whom, sainted in 2019? Composer Edward Elgar and film director Alfred Hitchcock share what connection with the church?

7 On this route, what is the name of the only London Underground station with none of the letters from the word 'mackerel' in its name?

8 The Grace Gate marks the main entrance to which major building very close to this route?

9 Canals are so cohesively woven into the fabric of a neighbourhood on this route that the area came to be called what?

You might notice distinctive green, wooden huts in various locations around London, with a line of cabs parked outside. These are cabmen's shelters, introduced in 1875 by the Earl of Shaftesbury. He was fed up with being unable to get a cab in bad weather because his local cabbies (whose drivers' seats in those days were open to the elements) would all be doing a little too much sheltering in the pub.

In a popular tradition dating back to the mid-nineteenth century, a swimming race is conducted in the icy waters of the Serpentine Lake on Christmas Day morning each year.

A hidden nook near the altar in Brompton Oratory was used as a 'dead letter drop' by Russian spies during the Cold War. It was easy for agents to lose a tail in nearby Harrods, with its crowds of shoppers and multitudinous exits.

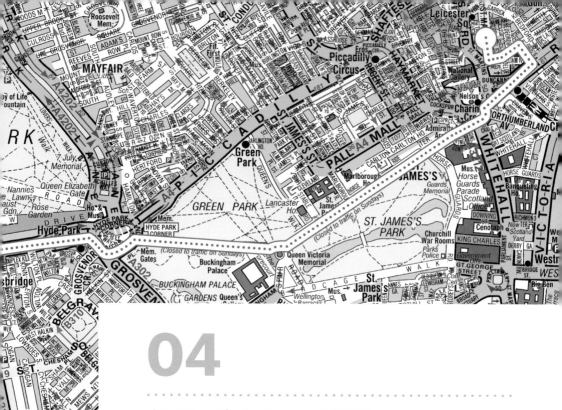

04

St Martin's Lane, WC2
to Fulham Broadway Station, SW6

Leave by William IV Street, left Chandos Place, right Bedford Street, right Strand, forward Charing Cross, comply King Charles I roundabout, leave by The Mall, forward Admiralty Arch, forward The Mall, right Queen's Gardens, forward Constitution Hill, forward Duke of Wellington Place, right Grosvenor Place, left Knightsbridge, bear left and bear left Brompton Road, forward Fulham Road, set down on the right

1   On your left towards the bottom of St Martin's Lane, you pass London's largest what? Designed by architect Frank Matcham and built in 1904, what is its name?

2   The equestrian statue of King Charles I on the roundabout between Whitehall and Trafalgar Square stands on the site of the original Charing Cross. What does this spot officially mark?

3   On your right towards the western end of The Mall is Clarence House. Who lived here from 1953 until 2002? Who lives here now?

4   On the north side of Hyde Park Corner is a building called Apsley House. It was the London home of who, in the nineteenth century? On account of it once being the first house in the city on the approach from Kensington, this building famously garnered what grand nickname?

5   In Brompton Road you pass London's largest what on the left? What is its name? What London first – with smelling salts on offer for those who dared experience it – was installed within in 1901?

6   Halfway between questions 1 and 5, you also passed London's largest what? What is its name?

7   You pass the home ground of which football club on your right on the approach to Fulham Broadway? What is the name of the ground?

8 This route took you past the only London Underground station with six consecutive consonants in its name. What is it called?

9 In which street on this route is the Royal Marsden Hospital? It is a world-leading centre in the treatment of what?

10 Which street on this route is so named because it was where King Charles II liked to go walking?

The narrowest alleyway in London is Brydges Place. Running between St Martin's Lane and Bedfordbury, at its narrowest point it is a mere 38 cm (15 in) wide.

In trade slang, 'roasting' is to sit on a taxi rank for a very long time waiting for a job – and of course, the longer you've waited, the harder it is to cut your losses and go. This is an all-too-common frustration during 'Kipper Season' (see page 90).

05

The Boltons, SW10
to Campden Hill Square, W8

Leave by Boltons Place, forward Bolton Gardens, forward Collingham Gardens, forward Collingham Road, left Cromwell Road, right Marloes Road, right Cheniston Gardens, left Wrights Lane, left Kensington High Street, right Campden Hill Road, left Aubrey Walk, right Hillsleigh Road, left into Campden Hill Square

1 A five-bedroomed, semi-detached house in Cresswell Place, next to the Boltons, was the fourth most expensive house bought in London in 2018. How much did it cost? How many brand-new London taxis could you buy for the same money at the time?

2 On your left at the top of Bolton Place is Bousfield Primary School. Why might it interest Beatrix Potter fans? Potter is thought to have taken inspiration for many of her characters' names from which site a little southwest of here?

3 Also just down Old Brompton Road from the Boltons is legendary Earls Court music venue the Troubadour, opened in 1954. Who made an early UK appearance here in December 1962, under the alias Blind Boy Grunt?

4 To the east along Kensington High Street from the point at which you cross it, is the home of the Duke and Duchess of Cambridge. What is its name?

5 In the same direction along the High Street you'll find the offices of which London newspaper? Which national daily newspaper also has offices here?

6 Which major museum relocated to Kensington High Street just to the west of here in 2016, having previously occupied a disused warehouse near Tower Bridge? Blockbuster exhibitions have included subjects ranging from Cartier watches and Ferrari cars to the architecture of Moscow and the films of Stanley Kubrick.

7 Holland Park, to your left as you drive up Campden Hill Road, is home to annual summer-season performances of what?

8 The area immediately north of Campden Hill Square is probably most famous for an event that takes place each August bank holiday weekend. What is it? Who starred as a fictional UK prime minister in a 1999 film set in and named after the area? And what is the name of the colourful antique and bric-a-brac street market held here?

9 Which major road on this route was named after the son of seventeenth-century Lord Protector of the Commonwealth of England, Scotland and Ireland, who had a house nearby?

06

Australia High Commission, WC2 to Paddington Station, W2

Leave on the right Strand, right Aldwych, left Drury Lane, left High Holborn, forward St Giles High Street, right Earnshaw Street, left New Oxford Street, forward Oxford Street, right Orchard Street, left Portman Square, forward Seymour Street, right Edgware Road, left Harrow Road, comply Bishop's Bridge roundabout, leave by Bishop's Bridge Road, left and comply Station Forecourt, set down on the left

1 Soon after setting off, you pass the northern end of which bridge over the River Thames, famous thanks to its position on a bend in the river that offers equally excellent views of Westminster and the City? What is the bridge's connection to Napoleon Bonaparte, the *Eurovision Song Contest*, and Terry and Julie?

2 Drury Lane's most famous building is the Theatre Royal, the back of which is on your left shortly after you turn off Aldwych. But the theatre's address isn't actually Drury Lane at all. In which street will you find the main entrance?

3 Travelling west down Oxford Street, which three London Underground stations do you pass? Which line do they all serve?

4 In 1921 English composer Edward Elgar opened which iconic music brand's first store, marked by a plaque on your left on Oxford Street, near the junction with Davies Street?

5 Unmissable on your right as you turn into Orchard Street are landmark premises opened in 1909 by Harry Gordon who, the establishment being named after him?

6 Orchard Street becomes a more famous street a little further north. What is its name? Who was the street's most famous (fictional) resident? At what number did he live?

7 Which landmark stands at the southern end of Edgware Road? For what was this site famous for six hundred years until 1783?

8 Why will you find a round-the-clock police guard outside a house just off this part of Edgware Road, in Connaught Square?

9 Sharing his surname with a London Underground station on this route, who wrote the famous series of children's books about a bear from Peru who turns up lost at Paddington Station? And which great Victorian engineer built Paddington Station in 1854?

07

Parliament Square, SW1
to Golden Lane, EC1

Leave by Bridge Street, left Victoria Embankment, left Temple Place, left Arundel Street, left Strand, right Melbourne Place, right Aldwych, left Strand, forward Fleet Street, left Fetter Lane, forward New Fetter Lane, forward Holborn Circus, leave by Charterhouse Street, right Lindsey Street, left Long Lane, forward Beech Street, left into Golden Lane

1 Who occupies the office building opened in 2001, seen on your left as you turn the corner from Bridge Street into the Victoria Embankment? What is the building's exterior designed to resemble, and why?

2 On your right at the same spot, what is Big Ben?

3 The Victoria Embankment was constructed in the nineteenth century, as part of major works to shore up the city against the tidal River Thames, to ease congestion in the Strand and Fleet Street, and to create a much-needed network of underground tunnels for what? Who was the engineer behind the scheme, memorialised in a bust nearby?

4 Which monument, on your right as you drive along the Victoria Embankment, was originally constructed in Egypt around 1450 BCE? What is erroneous about the way it was installed in London?

5   To your left here, looms Shell-Mex House, crowned by London's largest what? Where is London's second largest, also on this route?

6   What structure would have spanned the river to your right as you turn into Temple Place, had it not been abandoned in 2017 under public and financial pressure?

7   From what does Fleet Street take its name? With what industry – now long gone – is it synonymous?

8   Who reportedly had notorious premises at 186 Fleet Street in the eighteenth century? Which writer – coiner of the famous epigram, 'When a man is tired of London he is tired of life' – had a house in Gough Square, just off Fetter Lane? What seminal work did he create here?

9   Which complex of buildings around Beech Street, housing high-rise flats and a major arts centre, was built in the 1960s brutalist style by architects Chamberlin, Powell and Bon?

10 Where on this route is the only great London wholesale market still operating in the central part of the city? What is bought and sold there? The ancient field for which the market is named was the site of a fair for centuries. What name did the fair share with a nearby hospital?

11 Which two streets on this route are named after a priory dating back to 1348? In one of them you'll find Florin Court, an art deco apartment building that was used for exterior shots of the home of which fictional detective in a long-running television series?

08

**Armoury House, EC1
to Tower Bridge, SE1**

Leave on the right City Road, forward Finsbury Square, forward Finsbury Pavement, left South Place, forward Eldon Street, right Blomfield Street, left London Wall, forward Wormwood Street, forward Camomile Street, left Outwich Street, forward Houndsditch, left St Botolph Street, right Middlesex Street, right Aldgate High Street, left Minories, left Goodmans Yard, right Mansell Street, forward Tower Bridge Approach, forward onto Tower Bridge

1   Armoury House and the surrounding fields have been home to the Honourable Artillery Company since 1642. It was also home to London's original club in which sport?

2   Who lived and preached across the road from the Honourable Artillery Company in the late eighteenth century? What movement of the Christian Church did he found?

3   Where, near the start of this route, are William Blake, John Bunyan, Daniel Defoe, and the mother of the answer to question 2 buried? What links their – and thousands of other – burials in this place?

4   As you turn right into Blomfield Street, which building looms above you, south of London Wall in Old Broad Street? Opened in 1980 as the National Westminster (NatWest) Tower, it held what national distinction until the completion of One Canada Square, Canary Wharf, in 1991? What is distinctive about the building when viewed from above?

5   Which ditch is recalled in the name Houndsditch?

6   Dating from the late eleventh century, what is the name of the oldest part of the Tower of London, and who built it? In August 1941 Josef Jakobs was the last man to be executed at the Tower of London. What was his crime? Who were the last two people to be imprisoned here, in 1952? What was their crime?

7   In December 1952 bus driver Albert Gunter earned his place in London lore when he did what on Tower Bridge?

8   Which tourist attraction, over which Tower Bridge offers splendid views, played a critical role in the D-Day Normandy landings. What is its connection with the London Gateway services on the M1?

9   Around which two modern streets on this route might you have found wild medicinal plants growing in the Middle Ages?

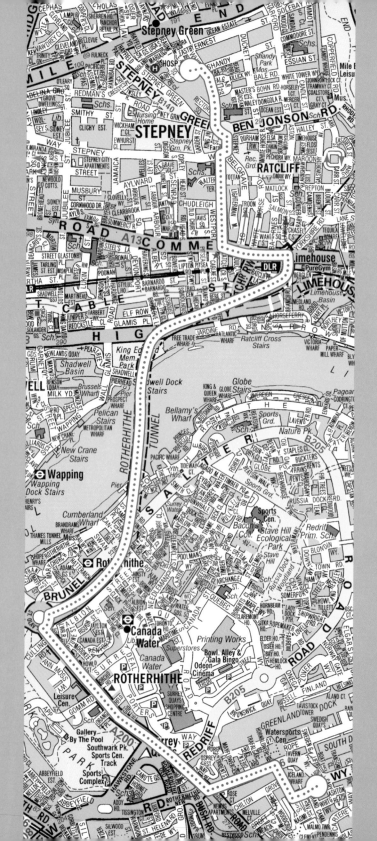

09

**Beaumont Square, E1
to Cannon Wharf Business
Centre, SE8**

*Leave on the right White Horse Lane, left Stepney Green,
comply roundabout, leave by Stepney High Street, comply
roundabout, leave by Stepney Way, left Bromley Street,
left Commercial Road, right Branch Road, forward Tunnel
Approach, forward Rotherhithe Tunnel, forward Tunnel
Approach, comply roundabout, leave by Lower Road, left
Plough Way, right Yeoman Street, left Pell Street, set down
on the left*

1   Just west of Beaumont Square in Mile End Road, a blue plaque marks
the site of the last London home of which explorer, who died in Hawaii
in 1779? And whose first children's home, opened in 1870, is marked by
another blue plaque just east of Stepney Green, in Ben Jonson Road?

2   1950s Stepney is the setting for which memoir by Jennifer Worth, made
into a hit BBC drama broadcast throughout the 2010s?

3 The Limehouse area along the River Thames was the original home of which immigrant community, now more readily associated with an area in the West End?

4 Which canal meets the River Thames at Limehouse Basin, having passed through Regent's Park, Camden, Angel and Hackney along its 13.8-km (8.6-mile) route through North London?

5 What declaration was signed in Narrow Street, in January 1981, by politicians Roy Jenkins, David Owen, Bill Rodgers and Shirley Williams? How were they collectively known? What did the declaration lead to the creation of?

6 The engineer who built the Rotherhithe Tunnel is memorialised in the name of which nearby street? Why was the tunnel constructed with two bends, one towards each end?

7 Timber from the ship the *Temeraire* was used for some of the furniture in St Mary's, Rotherhithe. Which great London painter memorialised the *Temeraire*'s final journey by tug to be broken up?

8 Who set sail from a jetty close to a pub now called the Mayflower in Rotherhithe Street in 1620?

9 Which location near this route got its name from the whaling ships that once berthed there?

10

Jubilee Gardens, SE1
to Royal London Hospital, E1

Leave on the left Belvedere Road, forward Upper Ground, right Broadwall, left Stamford Street, left Blackfriars Road, right Queen Victoria Street, forward Bank Junction, leave by Cornhill, forward Leadenhall Street, forward Aldgate, forward Aldgate High Street, forward Whitechapel High Street, forward Whitechapel Road, right New Road, left Stepney Way, set down on the left

1 Which municipal body had its home in County Hall on the river, just behind you as you begin this route, until its abolishment in 1986? What does the old County Hall building house now?

2 What is the United Kingdom's most popular paid tourist attraction, on your left as you begin this route? When it was opened in 2000 it was the world's tallest what?

3 From which festival do the Festival Pier and the Royal Festival Hall take their names?

4 The architect of which building on this stretch of the South Bank used innovative window design to get around planning rules on advertising, creating a much-loved London icon in the process?

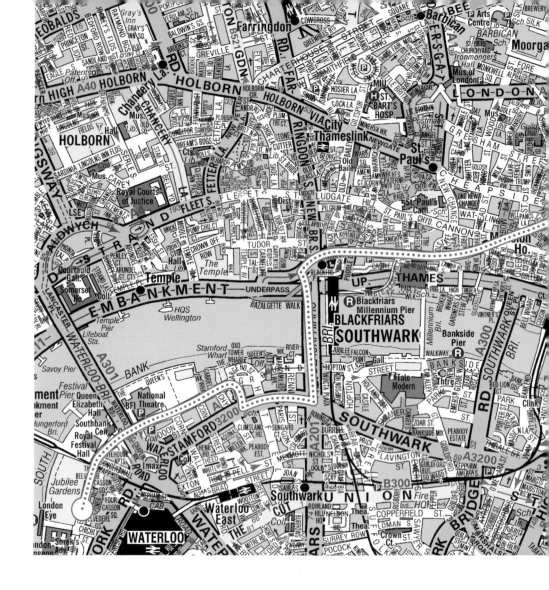

5 The junction of Queen Victoria Street and Peter's Hill is a good spot
to take in modern London's contrasting architectural styles, with
St Paul's Cathedral to your left and, to your right, a clear line of sight
to the river and which bridge, and which art gallery across it? When
did the bridge open, and why did it quickly close again? And what was
the original function of the building that houses the art gallery? After
completion of an extension in 2016, who did the gallery's director, Sir
Nicholas Serota, advise to 'get net curtains'?

6 What is the Old Lady of Threadneedle Street?

7 On your right, just off Whitechapel Road in Fieldgate Street as you approach the hospital, is the Whitechapel Bell Foundry, operational on this site since 1738. What is the name of perhaps the most famous bell cast here, housed in a tower a couple of miles to the west? Which other bell, cast here in 1752, can be seen at the Independence National Historical Park in Philadelphia?

8 One of the Royal London Hospital's most famous patients was played on screen by John Hurt in a 1980 film directed by David Lynch. What was his name, and his nickname, which was also the name of the film?

9 The name of which street on this route derives from its function as a spot where weary medieval travellers into the City of London could stop for a mug of beer?

10 Which street near this route – famous for its curry houses – gave its name to a 2003 novel by Monica Ali (and a film adaptation in 2007)?

11

Victoria Station, SW1 to Liverpool Street Station, EC2

Leave on the left Terminus Place, left Buckingham Palace Road, right Eccleston Street, right Eaton Square, forward Hobart Place, forward Lower Grosvenor Place, left Buckingham Palace Road, forward and left Buckingham Gate, forward Queen's Gardens, leave by The Mall, forward Admiralty Arch, forward The Mall, comply King Charles I roundabout, leave by Trafalgar Square East Side, right Duncannon Street, left Strand, bear left Aldwych, bear left Strand, forward Fleet Street, forward Ludgate Circus, forward Ludgate Hill, left Old Bailey, right Newgate Street, left King Edward Street, forward Little Britain, forward Montague Street, comply Rotunda, leave by London Wall, left Moorgate, right South Place, left Wilson Street, right Sun Street, left Appold Street, right Primrose Street, right Harwich Lane, set down facing ·

A favourite cabbie shortcut from John Adam Street in Charing Cross to the Embankment – Lower Robert Street – is known as 'the Batcave'. The open-air street suddenly disappears under buildings into what looks like a private parking garage, turns a sudden corner and comes out on the other side of the Savoy Hotel.

1   In Oscar Wilde's 1895 play *The Importance of Being Earnest*, what ladies' accessory is found in the cloakroom at Victoria Station?

2   The fictional Bellamy family lived just off Eaton Square at 165 Eaton Place in which classic ITV series? And in which post-war British film comedy is the area just south of Buckingham Palace Road ceded from the United Kingdom?

3   The Mall was created in the late seventeenth century by which monarch? It replaced Pall Mall as a new course for playing which game?

4   Bush House, on your right as you head around the semicircle of Aldwych, served as the headquarters of which media service from 1941 to 2012?

5   Ludgate Hill is famous for its approach view of which London landmark?

6   Which hospital stood in what is now Liverpool Street from 1247 until 1676, when it moved to Moorfields? How has its name become part of the English language?

It is a long tradition
in the taxi trade that a
new driver's first fare is
given free or donated
to charity – usually
**Great Ormond Street
Hospital for children.**

7 What is the name of the
bronze statue by Israeli
sculptor Frank Meisler that stands
outside Liverpool Street Station.
It commemorates the arrival here of
which group of people in the late 1930s?

8 Which street on this route marks the northern boundary of ancient
Roman London?

9 Who is memorialised by two buildings, one statue and two streets on,
or very close, to this route?

**One Knowledge
examiner was renowned
for choosing the start and
end points of his questions by
throwing darts at a map. If the
student felt this was unfair
they were invited to throw
the darts themselves.**

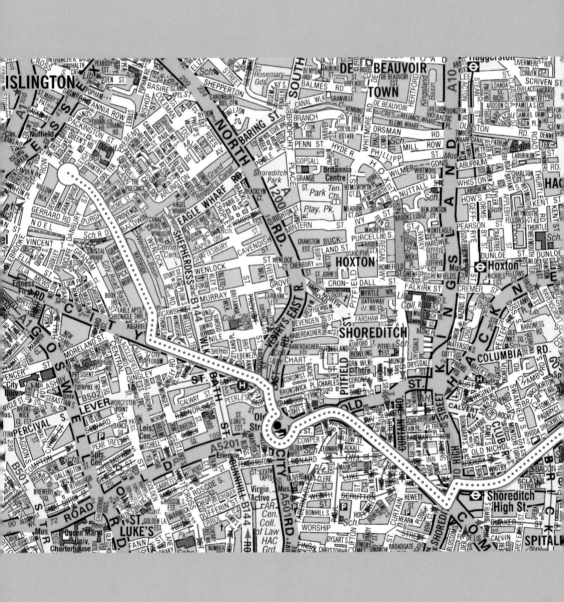

12

Bancroft Road, E1
to St Peter's Street, N1

Leave on the right Globe Road, left Roman Road, forward Bethnal Green Road, left Shoreditch High Street, right Great Eastern Street, forward Old Street, comply St Agnes Well, leave by City Road, right Wharf Road, forward into St Peter's Street

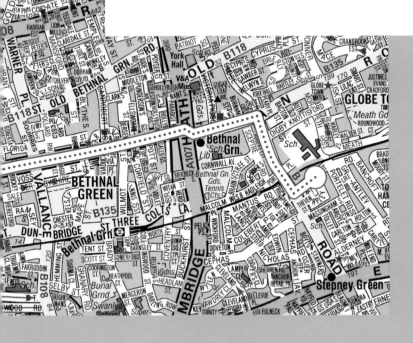

1 Just east of Bancroft Road, a blue
   plaque on the railway bridge in
   Grove Road marks the site of the first
   occurrence of what, on 13th June 1944?

2 Just west of Bancroft Road, at the junction
   of Cambridge Heath Road and Whitechapel
   Road, the Blind Beggar pub commemorates the local
   legend of Henry de Montfort, who lost his sight at the Battle of
   Evesham in 1265 and is supposed to have begged at this crossroads.
   Also at this spot, in the late nineteenth century, William Booth preached
   his first open-air sermons before setting up the East London Christian
   Mission, which went on to become what? And who shot George Cornell
   inside the pub in 1966?

3 Which park close to the start of this route was partly made up of land
   that once belonged to the Bishop of London? Which nearby streetname
   reflects this?

4 To what tragedy of March 1943 does the Stairway to Heaven memorial
   above the entrance to Bethnal Green Underground station pay tribute?

5 The horse-drawn funeral corteges of which three brothers attracted
   thousands of spectators to Bethnal Green Road in March 1995 and April
   and October 2000?

6 In Victorian times, immediately to your north as you approach
   Shoreditch High Street, was a notorious what, known as the Old Nichol
   and fictionalised as the Jago in an 1896 novel by Arthur Morrison?

7 Immediately to the north of here, which street is famous for its colourful Sunday morning flower market?

8 The area around the junction of Old Street and City Road has, in recent times, acquired what nickname, in a nod to the many digital start-up firms in the vicinity? Why, since summer 2019, is the nickname technically inaccurate?

9 In City Road, as you pass the junction with Shepherdess Walk, you see a pub on your right that features in a famous nursery rhyme. What's the name of the pub? And the nursery rhyme?

10 Just west of St Peter's Street is Angel Underground station. What distinction do its escalators hold? What gave Angel its name, and what, therefore, makes it unique on the Monopoly board? And how is all this connected to a plaque inside the branch of the Co-operative Bank at the corner of Islington High Street and Pentonville Road?

Stage 2:

The
28s

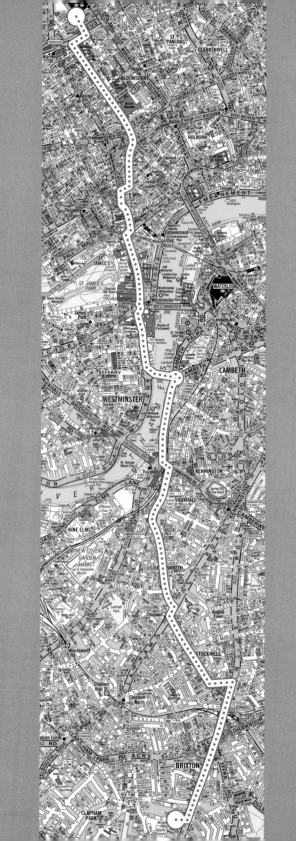

01

➤➤

Euston Station, NW1
to Brixton Prison, SW2

---

*Leave on the left Melton Street, forward Gordon Street, right
Gower Place, left Gower Street, forward Bedford Square, forward
Bloomsbury Street, forward Shaftesbury Avenue, forward
Princes Circus, leave by Shaftesbury Avenue, left Monmouth
Street, comply Seven Dials, leave by Monmouth Street, forward
Upper St Martin's Lane, right Cranbourn Street, left Charing
Cross Road, forward St Martin's Place, forward Trafalgar Square
East Side, comply King Charles I Island, leave by Whitehall,
forward Parliament Street, comply Parliament Square, leave by
St Margaret Street, forward Old Palace Yard, forward Abingdon
Street, forward Millbank, comply Millbank Circus, leave by
Lambeth Bridge, comply Lambeth Circus, leave by Albert
Embankment, left Kennington Lane, right and bear left South
Lambeth Road, left Stockwell Terrace, right Clapham Road, left
Stockwell Road, left Stockwell Park Walk, right Brixton Road,
forward Brixton Hill, right Jebb Avenue, facing Brixton Prison*

1   A pub outside Euston Station, named the Doric Arch, commemorates
which arch, demolished in 1961?

2   In October 1814, eight people in the area just east of Princes Circus – then
     a notorious slum – were killed in a flood of what, originating from which
     premises in Tottenham Court Road? Which theatre now stands here?

3   The same slum is the setting for William Hogarth's famous engraving
     of a street scene that features a drunken mother absent-mindedly
     dropping her suckling baby to its death. What's the engraving called?
     And what was the name of the slum? Visible in the background is the
     distinctive spire of which Bloomsbury church?

4   Which street in Lambeth is named after the eldest son of Edward III?

5   A blue plaque at 87 Hackford Road in Stockwell records the residence
     here of which artist in the 1870s, while working for a Dutch art dealer?

6   What unusual visitor attraction – a remnant of the area's rural past –
     can be found just off Blenheim Gardens in Brixton?

7   Which philosopher – then aged 89 – spent seven days in Brixton Prison
     after his arrest for breach of the peace while attending a demonstration
     against nuclear weapons in September 1961? Six years later, which rock
     star was sentenced to three months here for possession of amphetamines?

8   The old governor's house at Brixton Prison houses The Clink, rated on
     internet comparison sites as one of London's top what?

9   Just off Brixton Road, a mural of which one-time local became the focus
     of candlelit vigils in January 2016, after his death in New York aged 69?

10   At which institution on this route did former Kenyan president Jomo
     Kenyatta spend time in the mid-1930s?

02

Overhill Road, SE22
to Marylebone Station, NW1

*Leave by Underhill Road, forward Whateley Road, right Lordship
Lane, comply Goose Green roundabout, leave by Grove Vale,
forward Dog Kennel Hill, forward Grove Lane, left Champion
Park, right Denmark Hill, left Camberwell New Road, forward
Harleyford Street, forward Kennington Oval, forward Harleyford
Road, left South Lambeth Road, right Parry Street, right
Wandsworth Road, left Bridge Foot, forward Vauxhall Bridge,
forward Bessborough Gardens, forward Vauxhall Bridge Road, left
Neathouse Place, right Wilton Road, left Victoria Street, forward
and right Grosvenor Gardens, forward Grosvenor Place, right
Hyde Park Corner, left Park Lane, left Cumberland Gate, right
Marble Arch, left Great Cumberland Place, left Seymour Street,
right Seymour Place, right York Street, left Enford Street, forward
Harewood Avenue, right Melcombe Place, set down on the left*

1   A plaque at 163 Denmark Hill records it was once home to which
    influential nineteenth-century art critic? He is also memorialised in the
    name of what, nearby?

2 Which organisation has its headquarters at the foot of Vauxhall Bridge and why has it featured in several films from a popular British franchise?

3 In Hyde Park, just off the southern end of Park Lane, fifty-two stainless-steel pillars stand as a memorial to the victims of which unhappy event in recent history? You'll also find a memorial to which casualties of war in Brook Gate, leading to Brook Street off the northern end of Park Lane?

4 Further down Brook Street, at numbers 23 and 25, are two blue plaques to two immigrant musicians who lived here 250 years apart. Their homes are preserved and open as a museum bearing both of their names - who were they? Which hotel was established a few doors down in 1812?

5 Which architect constructed Marble Arch as an entrance to which landmark London building? In the week before Easter 2019, the gyratory around Marble Arch became impassable to traffic. Why?

6 What inconvenience first befell London motorists in Great Cumberland Place in September 1960?

7 Marylebone was originally named after which river, which ran through what is now Marylebone Lane, Marble Arch and Park Lane on its way to the River Thames? Why were locals keen to rename the area?

8 A hit Channel 4 television show is mainly filmed at an institution on this route. Name both the show and the institution.

9 Which area on this route has a butterfly named after it?

10 For much of the twentieth century, a Methodist minister was a regular attraction near this route. Where, and what was his name?

03

**Lorrimore Square, SE17
to Old Bailey, EC4**

*Leave by Chapter Road, leave by Carter Street, left and right
Penrose Street, left Walworth Road, comply Elephant and
Castle, leave by Newington Causeway, forward Borough
High Street, left Great Suffolk Street, left Surrey Row, right
Blackfriars Road, forward Blackfriars Bridge, forward New
Bridge Street, left Bridewell Place, right Tudor Street, right
Whitefriars Street, right Fleet Street, forward Ludgate Circus,
forward Ludgate Hill, left into Old Bailey*

1 John Smith House, on your right as you head up Walworth Road
towards Elephant and Castle, was the headquarters of which
organisation from 1980 to 1997?

2 The controversial high-rise Strata building at Elephant and Castle
houses three wind turbines at its summit that the architects intended to
provide eight per cent of the building's electricity. In fact, they provide
almost none because they are rarely turned on – why? What dubious
architectural award did Strata win after its completion in 2010?

3 The Black Friar pub, at the junction of Queen Victoria Street and New Bridge Street, occupies a small part of the site of which medieval institution? It is the only example of which decorative architectural style among London pubs?

4 The walled Temple area, in front of you at the end of Tudor Street, is home to which profession? From what does Temple take its name?

5 An institution on Old Bailey has taken the street's name, but what is it called officially? A bronze statue depicting who or what crowns its roof? And which notorious prison, named after a Roman entrance to the City, stood on this site for centuries until its last incarnation was demolished in 1902?

6 What are the names of the other two crown courts this route passes?

7 In the Middle Ages, where near this route would you have found Paul's Walk – a food and livestock market as well as a haunt of local prostitutes?

8 Until the Great Fire of London in 1666, an oddly named church near this route had a royal storehouse as its neighbour. Both were destroyed in the fire, but only the church rebuilt – what is its name?

9 A tomb near this route bears the Latin inscription, '*Lector si monumentum requiris circumspice*' – usually translated as, 'Reader, if you seek his monument, look around you'. Whose tomb, and where is it? This location has been closed just once since the Blitz – in 2011. Why?

10 In the thirteenth century, to whom did Edward I give permission to knock down a southern portion of the London Wall so that they could extend their accommodation?

04

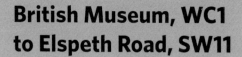

British Museum, WC1 to Elspeth Road, SW11

Leave on the right Great Russell Street, left Bloomsbury Street, forward Shaftesbury Avenue, forward Princes Circus, leave by Shaftesbury Avenue, forward Cambridge Circus, forward Shaftesbury Avenue, left Great Windmill Street, forward Haymarket, right Charles II Street, left Waterloo Place, right Pall Mall, comply roundabout, leave by Marlborough Gate, forward Marlborough Road, right The Mall, left Queen's Gardens, forward Spur Road, right Birdcage Walk, forward Buckingham Gate, forward Buckingham Palace Road, right Pimlico Road, forward Royal Hospital Road, right Chelsea Embankment, left Albert Bridge, forward Albert Bridge Road, right Cambridge Road, left Battersea Bridge Road, forward Latchmere Road, forward into Elspeth Road

1   The British Museum opened in the mid-eighteenth century, thanks to a bequest from whom? He lived in which part of London, where several streets and which famous square are named after him?

2   Which two famous West End districts are on your left and right as you drive down Shaftesbury Avenue between Cambridge Circus and Great Windmill Street?

3 Which show ran for more than thirty-three years at the Queen's Theatre, Shaftesbury Avenue, until it closed for refurbishment in July 2019 – making it the West End's longest continuously running musical? The theatre reopened the same year – under what new name, and with what show?

4 Shortly after turning right into Pall Mall, you pass the Reform Club on the left. What is its famous connection to nineteenth-century adventure literature? You then pass the Royal Automobile Club, also on the left. Which London Underground line reportedly runs 5 m (16 ft) below the bottom of the club's swimming pool? Between which two stations?

5 Where on this route did Charles I spend his last night alive?

6 Royal Hospital Road is named for the magnificent Royal Hospital, on your left. Who was its architect? Who lives here? And which world-famous event takes place in the grounds each summer?

7 As you turn right into Chelsea Embankment you have a fine view of the River Thames, looking west towards Albert and Battersea bridges. Which great English Romantic painter – who built an attic studio to make the most of the river light and sunsets – lived out his final years just beyond Battersea Bridge? A notice at the entrance to Albert Bridge instructs whom to do what, and why?

8 Which saint – who lived in a house on this stretch of the river until his arrest in 1534 – is commemorated by a large seated statue in the grounds of nearby Chelsea Old Church?

9 As you cross Lavender Hill and enter Elspeth Road, a much-loved local cultural institution is on your left, housed in what was once Battersea Town Hall. What is its name?

05

Battersea Church Road, SW11 to Goodge Street Station, W1

Leave on the left Battersea Bridge Road, forward Battersea Bridge, forward Beaufort Street, right King's Road, comply Sloane Square, leave by Sedding Street, right Sloane Terrace, left D'Oyley Street, forward Cadogan Lane, right Pont Street, forward Chesham Place, comply Belgrave Square, leave by Grosvenor Crescent, left Grosvenor Place, right Hyde Park Corner, forward Piccadilly, left Down Street, right Hertford Street, right Curzon Street, left Queen Street Mayfair, right Charles Street, comply Berkeley Square, leave by Bruton Street, forward Conduit Street, left Regent Street, forward Oxford Circus, forward Regent Street, right Mortimer Street, forward Goodge Street, left Tottenham Court Road, set down on the left

1 On your left at the north end of Battersea Bridge is a statue of a nineteenth-century American artist who settled in London and took inspiration from this stretch of the River Thames. A small residential street nearby is named after him. Who is the artist, and what is the name of the street?

2 King's Road was originally a private road used by Charles II to commute between which two palaces - one in central London (no longer standing), the other now a major tourist attraction in a southwestern suburb?

3 On your right in King's Road, at the junction with Royal Avenue, is a branch of McDonald's. From the late 1960s to the late 1980s this building served as which iconic countercultural venue, featured in the Rolling Stones' classic song 'You Can't Always Get What You Want'?

4 Just west along King's Road from Beaufort Street is number 430, home to a famous boutique during the punk era - what was its name? Who were its two famous proprietors? Which band - sharing part of its name with that of the boutique - did one of them manage?

5 Which Belgravia concert hall that shares its name with several nearby streets is home to the Royal Philharmonic Orchestra and hosts chamber concerts during the annual BBC Proms festival?

6 From what does Piccadilly take its name?

7 Who, commemorated by a plaque on the wall of what is now Hakkasan restaurant, was born at 17 Bruton Street on 21st April 1926?

Beneath Buckingham Palace Road, south of Belgravia, are the remains of a Hurricane aeroplane. Having run out of ammunition, it knocked down a German bomber heading for the palace in 1940. The pilot parachuted to safety before his own plane then crashed.

8 In August 1889 at the Langham Hotel, Langham Place, ahead of you as you turn right into Mortimer Street, publisher Joseph Marshall Stoddart dined with two literary greats and commissioned pieces from both of them for his magazine. One wrote a detective story involving four convicts set in the 1857 Indian Rebellion, the other a scandalous society tale set in contemporary London. Both went on to become classics – name both the works and their authors.

9 Which corporation has its headquarters across the road from the Langham Hotel?

10 Which Square on this route features in a famous song written in the late 1930s that has since been recorded by countless artists including Vera Lynn, Nat King Cole and Rod Stewart? What's the name of the song?

11 Which street on this route is generally considered to mark the border between Soho and Mayfair?

The only statue of a royal mistress in London is that of Charles II's beloved Nell Gwyn. It adorns the facade of an apartment block named after her near King's Road.

06

. . . .

Tilling Road, NW2
to Chetwynd Road, NW5

. . . .

Leave by Brentfield Gardens, left Highfield Avenue, right Golders Green Road, forward North End Road, forward North End Way, comply roundabout, leave by North End Way, forward Heath Street, left East Heath Road, forward South End Road, forward South End Green, left Constantine Road, forward Agincourt Road, left Mansfield Road, forward Gordon House Road, forward into Chetwynd Road

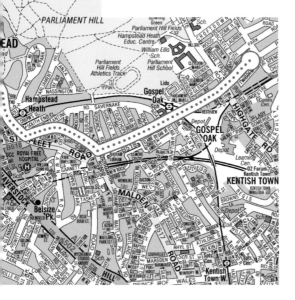

1   This route begins across the North Circular from which two British firsts? One, on the map, was opened in 1976. The other, just off the map, opened in 1959 and is connected how with Leeds?

2   Next door to Golders Green Underground station, the Centre for Islamic Enlightening is housed in a building that opened in 1913 as what? It played host to the likes of Arthur Askey and Chico Marx before being taken over by the BBC in 1969, after which it was used as a TV and radio concert venue and studio until 2003.

3   Who wrote the famous lines, 'My heart aches, and a drowsy numbness pains / My sense, as though of hemlock I had drunk', possibly while sitting in his garden just off South End Road? What is the name of the poem the couplet opens?

4   Who set up both home and practice at 20 Maresfield Gardens – now a museum – in Hampstead in 1938 after fleeing Nazi persecution in his native Austria? And what is his connection with a sleeping Job Centre employee from South London?

5   Which part of Hampstead Heath, just north of Hampstead Heath Underground station, is famous for its expansive views of London? One possible explanation for its name is that a group of conspirators gathered here to watch their labours (fail to) come to fruition – who were they?

6 The junction of South Hill Park and South End Road was the site of a shooting, the consequence of which saw the last what take place at Holloway Prison in 1955? Who committed the crime?

7 Hampstead Underground station holds what distinction, leading to its being earmarked as London Transport's headquarters in the event of a nuclear attack in the 1950s?

8 Which building on this route – once a coaching inn and now housing apartments and a health suite – is named after a leader of the Peasant's Revolt of 1381? According to legend, he took refuge here before his capture and execution.

9 Which two colourful MPs held parliamentary seats on this route at the turn of the twenty-first century, and in which constituencies? Each also had another, higher-profile job. What was it?

North End tube station, between Golders Green and Hampstead on the Northern Line and buried deep under Hampstead Heath, was built in the mid 1900s but has never operated due to successful campaigning to preserve the wild parkland above it.

07

Well Street, E9
to Finsbury Park Station, N4

Leave on the right Mare Street, left Richmond Road, right Greenwood Road, left Graham Road, forward Dalston Lane, forward Balls Pond Road, right Mildmay Park, comply Newington Green, leave by Green Lanes, left Riversdale Road, right Mountgrove Road, right Blackstock Road, left Rock Street, right St Thomas's Road, forward Station Place, set down on the left

1 Why did a video of walking-stick-
   wielding local resident Pauline
   Pierce go viral in the summer of
   2011, earning her the nickname
   'the heroine of Hackney'?

2 Who opened a refuge 'for affording
   temporary food and shelter for destitute
   females on their discharge from the
   Metropolitan gaols' at 195 Mare Street in 1860?

3 Hackney's oldest buildings – the Tudor home of Sir Ralph Sadleir
   (Sutton House) and the sixteenth-century tower of St Augustine's
   Church – stand near the northern end of Mare Street. Only the tower of
   St Augustine's was kept when the old church was demolished. Why?
   What is the name of the replacement church that now stands next to
   the original tower? Ralph Sadleir was Henry VIII's secretary of state
   from 1540 to 1543 – who was his predecessor in the job? Both men and
   Sadleir's Hackney home feature in a successful series of twenty-first-
   century novels by which author?

4 A blue plaque at 55 Graham Road, just north of Richmond Road, marks
   the 1890s home of which performer, fondly known as the 'Queen of the
   Music Hall'?

5 Fassett Square, in Dalston, was the blueprint for which fictional square? That square itself is in which fictional district, named after a road a little further north, in Stoke Newington?

6 Just off Dalston Lane, in Beechwood Road you'll find Holy Trinity Church, home to an unusual tradition in which members of what profession attend an annual service in full costume and give a free performance for local children afterwards? A banner in the church proclaims, 'Here we are fools for Christ', and a stained-glass window, along with the biblical quotation, 'A time to weep, a time to laugh, a time to mourn, a time to dance', depicts whom?

7 Just north of Newington Green, in Nevill Road, a plaque on the wall of a now-residential building records that it was once a pub – the Nevill Arms. An event occurred for the first time in London, in the garden of this pub, on 30th May 1915. What event?

8 A large communal garden overlooked by four luxury, gated apartment blocks just off Blackstock Road played what role from 1913 to 2006?

9 A park near this route is popular with open-air swimmers and gave its name to an acclaimed comic novel published in 1989. Name both the park and the author of the novel. Which nearby street houses a popular Saturday market by day and becomes a fashionable hang-out by night?

08

Cambridge Heath Station, E2 to Mudchute Station, E14

Leave on the right Cambridge Heath Road, left Roman Road, right Globe Road, left Mile End Road, right White Horse Lane, comply roundabout, leave by Stepney High Street, forward Belgrave Street, left Troon Street, forward Salmon Lane, left Commercial Road, right West India Dock Road, right Westferry Road, comply Westferry Circus Lower Tier, leave by Westferry Road, left Marsh Wall, right Limeharbour, forward East Ferry Road, set down on the right

1   The Isle of Dogs was once what kind of land, as commemorated by a street name on this route? What major industry was centred here in the nineteenth and early twentieth centuries? And what major industry is centred here now?

2   Which institution on the northern part of the Isle of Dogs had a history in the City of London going back to at least 1016 until it moved to its current premises in 1982? What is its business?

3 A public artwork by French sculptor Pierre Vivant sited on the Isle of Dogs - originally at Westferry Circus, now further east near the answer to question 2 - is made from what?

4 From what does Canary Wharf take its name?

5 A blue plaque towards the southern end of Westferry Road marks the launch site of which ship in 1858? At the time it was the largest ship in the world. Who designed it?

6 Mudchute's unusual name comes from its history as the spot that mud was deposited from where, in the late nineteenth century?

7 What unusual feature of the Docklands Light Railway (DLR) makes it popular with children? And which station served as the DLR's original Central London terminus?

8 Cubitt Town is named after which Cubitt, who built much of the housing in the area in the nineteenth century? What political office did he hold before his death in the 1860s? What were the names of his two more famous brothers, also London builders?

9 On which street in the Isle of Dogs will you find the Museum of London Docklands?

09

Parnell Road, E3
to North Greenwich Station, SE10

Leave on the left Tredegar Road, forward Wick Lane, right East Cross Route, forward Blackwall Tunnel Northern Approach, forward Blackwall Tunnel, forward Blackwall Tunnel Southern Approach, left Dreadnought Street, left Blackwall Lane, comply roundabout, leave by Millennium Way, comply roundabout, leave by station forecourt, set down on the left

1   Who, led by Annie Besant, went on strike in Fairfield Road, just south of Tredegar Road, in 1888?

2   Bow Creek is the name given to which river as it approaches the River Thames? The name 'Bow' comes from the Old English for which structure relating to the river?

3 On your right as you head down towards the Blackwall Tunnel, are two controversial 1960s housing schemes. The first, designed in the brutalist style by Erno Goldfinger, still stands. The second was designed by husband and wife architects Peter and Alison Smithson along Le Corbusier's 'Streets in the Sky' principles; named after a folk hero, it is now mainly demolished, although part of it has been saved for posterity by the Victoria & Albert Museum. Name the two developments.

4 Until the opening of what, in 1963, the Blackwall Tunnel had the distinction of being what?

5 A monument at Virginia Quay in Jamestown Way, just east of the northern entrance to the Blackwall Tunnel, pays tribute to the embarkation of whom from this spot, in 1606?

6 Greenwich Peninsula was once home to the world's largest what? And Greenwich Peninsula is now home to the world's largest what?

7 What would a ticket for Up at The O2 entitle you to do?

8 Just east of North Greenwich Underground station is the southern terminus for which controversial (and corporately branded) part of London's public transport network?

9 In November 2000, police foiled an attempt to steal £350 million of what, from where on this route?

Researchers from the University of London have established that the process of studying the Knowledge changes the shape of Knowledge boys' and girls' brains, increasing the size of the posterior hippocampus, which deals with spatial memory.

The quiet period at the beginning of the year, when there are fewer tourists and Londoners tend to hibernate – traditionally between the end of the January sales and the end of the Easter holidays – is known in the trade as 'Kipper Season'. The origins of this are unclear, but it may reference either being able to afford only the most basic foodstuffs during this period, or that business is 'flat'.

10

New Cross Station, SE14 to the National Maritime Museum, SE10

Leave on the left Amersham Vale, right Edward Street, left Deptford High Street, right Creek Road, left Greenwich Church Street, right College Approach, right King William Walk, left Romney Road, right Park Row, set down on the right

1 The 1997 film *Nil by Mouth*, much of which was filmed in and around New Cross, is loosely based on the youth of its writer and director, who was born here. What is his name?

2 Artists Bridget Riley, Lucian Freud, Antony Gormley, Damien Hirst and Steve McQueen are all alumni of which educational institution, based in New Cross?

3 Which Elizabethan playwright's glittering career came to a violent and premature end in a house near Deptford Creek, when he was stabbed in the face and killed during an argument in May 1593, aged just twenty-nine?

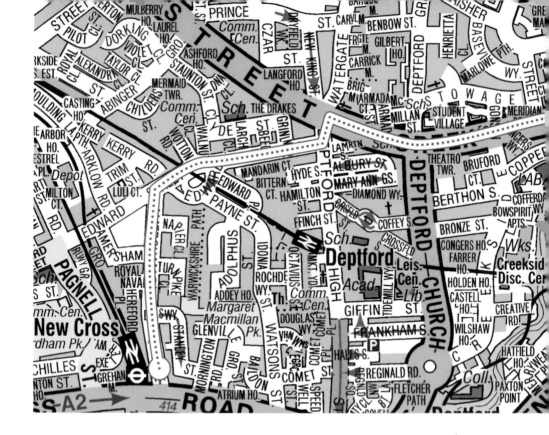

4   Deptford Creek is part of which River Thames tributary?

5   In 1577 Sir Francis Drake set sail around the world from Deptford – in which boat? In 1768 Captain Cook set sail from Deptford for Australia. What was his boat called?

6   As you turn the corner from Greenwich Church Street into College Approach, before you stands a beautifully preserved, dry-docked sailing clipper that was once the fastest means of transporting wool from Australia to London and is now a popular tourist attraction. What is the name of this boat?

7 As you drive along Romney Road, the magnificent Old Royal Naval College on your left is built on the site of which medieval palace? Which monarch was born there in 1491? And which famous architect designed the current buildings, originally built as a seaman's hospital between 1696 and 1712?

8 The National Maritime Museum is set within which Royal Park? What line of longitude is it on? What other attraction in the park provides the reason for this, and what is the purpose of the metal ball on a pole on its roof?

9 One of the National Maritime Museum's most prized exhibits is the coat worn by whom, and where, in 1805?

11

Consort Road, SE15 to the Ministry of Defence, SW1

Leave on the left Peckham High Street, right Peckham Hill Street, forward Willow Brook Road, forward Sumner Road, forward Trafalgar Avenue, left Old Kent Road, bear left New Kent Road, comply Elephant and Castle, leave by St George's Road, forward and left Westminster Bridge Road, forward Westminster Bridge, forward Bridge Street, comply Parliament Square, leave by Parliament Street, forward Whitehall, right Horseguards Avenue, set down on the right

. . . .

1 What was the name of the fake mineral water marketed by Del Boy after taking it from the tap in his council flat in the 1992 Christmas special of *Only Fools and Horses?*

2 Which iconic building looms directly in front of you – 3.2 km (2 miles) away – as you drive north up Peckham Hill Street?

3 Apart from being the first square after passing Go, what is unique about Old Kent Road on the Monopoly board? What did the Romans call Old Kent Road?

4 Which pioneering film actor and director was born near Elephant and Castle in 1889? Which other film actor – famous for his cockney accent – was born here in 1933?

5 What pivotal role has Gaunt Street, just north of Elephant and Castle, played in the London (and UK) clubbing scene since 1991?

6 In St George's Road, you pass which museum on your left? St George's Cathedral, on your right, played host to a historic first upon the visit of whom, in 1982?

7 What is the name of the memorial at the southern end of Whitehall? What annual commemorations are centred around it? Who designed it?

8 Why does the Ministry of Defence have an enormous wine cellar?

9 Who wrote 'Ne'er saw I, never felt, a calm so deep!', about standing where on this route?

12

Stamford Street, SE1 to Stamford Hill, N16

Leave by Southwark Street, left Borough High Street, forward London Bridge, forward King William Street, bear right Gracechurch Street, forward Bishopsgate, forward Norton Folgate, forward Shoreditch High Street, forward Kingsland Road, forward Kingsland High Street, forward Stoke Newington Road, forward Stoke Newington High Street, forward into Stamford Hill

1 Southwark in medieval and Elizabethan times – outside of the jurisdiction of the City on the north side of the Thames – was home to much of London's entertainment. A replica – opened in 1997 – of whose theatre stands close to its original site here? What nearby street name recalls a bloodier form of entertainment?

2 Which seventeenth-century Londoner lived in a house on this part of the river, and why was the view from this location important to him? What is odd about the plaque at 49 Bankside that records this information?

3 London Bridge was, for centuries, the only road crossing of the River Thames in central London until the opening of which other bridge in 1750? Traffic congestion on the medieval bridge led, in the eighteenth-century, to the introduction of what? The current London Bridge was opened in 1973 – what happened to the previous bridge?

4 What is the nickname of the distinctive skyscraper at 20 Fenchurch Street, which dominates the view to the north as you cross London Bridge? What inadvertent consequence of the building's unusual shape had to be urgently addressed during construction?

5 All of the streets on this route, from King William Street onwards, are part of which A-road, largely following the route of which Roman road from London to where?

6 Commemorated by both a blue plaque and the name of a nearby street, which eighteenth-century writer lived at 95 Stoke Newington Church Street?

7 Stamford Hill is known for its large population of which religious community?

8 The name of which area on this route recalls that it was once a place where animals could be tethered and watered?

9 Who was Catherine Booth, buried in Stoke Newington in 1890? Who was her husband? What was the name of the country house that once stood in the grounds of the cemetery that is their resting place?

10 With what place on this route do William Wallace, Sir Thomas More and Thomas Cromwell share an unfortunate connection?

Stage 3:

The 21s

➤➤

01

Torriano Avenue, NW5
to The Bishop's Avenue, N2

Leave on the left Leighton Road, right Kentish Town Road, left Highgate Road, comply roundabout, leave by Highgate West Hill, left The Grove, left Hampstead Lane, right into The Bishop's Avenue

1 Whose funeral cortege did Mary Shelley watch going past her window in Kentish Town Road in 1824?

2 How is Swain's Lane, running parallel to Highgate West Hill, connected with the Russian Revolution and a North London estate agent? What link do all of these share with a shop in Charing Cross Road?

3 Why, for several months from December 2017, was the small green at the corner of Highgate West Hill and The Grove awash with floral and written tributes?

4 In the 1970s, a series of sightings of what, where in Highgate, caused a media sensation?

5 What nickname is sometimes used to refer to The Bishop's Avenue, on account of its gargantuan houses (and their prices)? According to his 2012 memoir *Joseph Anton*, which author was obliged to live here for a time in the 1990s, and why?

6 A popular pub just south of the Bishop's Avenue was once a coaching inn frequented by an eighteenth-century criminal, who found it a good spot to suss out his targets. Who was he, and what's the name of the pub?

7 Winnington Road and Ingram Avenue, near the end of this route, are named after whom?

8 What does a mansion near this route have in common with much social housing throughout London, the United Kingdom and Ireland? What's the name of the mansion?

9 '. . . mostly lives up or down to its reputation, insufferably cosy details allied to a central blankness of imagination which shuffled the shops out to the edges, then refused to build a pub . . .' – these words from architecture critic Ian Nairn's classic, *Nairn's London*, refer to which area near this route? With which political party does the area have a longstanding connection? Several of the party's senior figures have lived here over the last century, including which prime minister and which grandson of which home secretary?

02

Crouch End Broadway, N4 to Spring Hill, N16

Leave by Crouch Hill, left Cecile Park, right Womersley Road, left Mount View Road, right Oakfield Road, left Endymion Road, right Green Lanes, left Woodberry Grove, left Seven Sisters Road, right Amhurst Park, forward Clapton Common, left into Spring Hill

1 It is thought that Crouch End's unusual name derives from one of two local historical landmarks, or possibly takes its name from both of them – what might they have been? The hilly roads in the area offer excellent views of which nearby landmark – itself on a hill a mile or so to the north – that opened in 1873?

2 According to urban legend, when Bob Dylan was recording in London in the 1980s, he knocked on the door of number 145 Crouch End Hill and asked, 'Is Dave here?' The Dave who happened to reside at this address – a local tradesman and Dylan fan – had just popped out, so his wife offered Bob a cup of tea while he waited. Shortly Dave returned and was amazed to find his hero sitting on the settee. Which Dave had Dylan actually been looking for? And at what address?

3 Which future politician lived briefly in Crouch End in the 1960s, between spells in New York, Oxford and Washington DC?

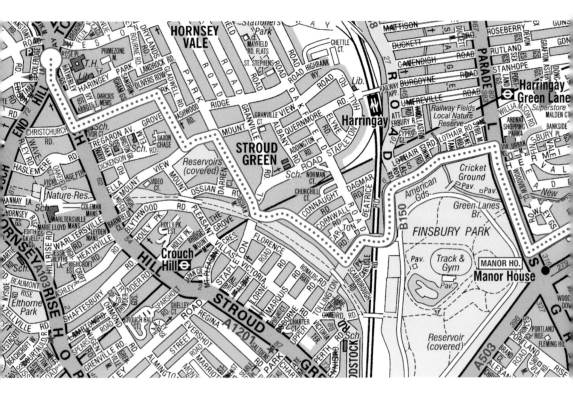

4 Which architect – famous for countless buildings in London's West End as well as in towns and cities across the United Kingdom – is commemorated by a blue plaque at his former home in Haslemere Road, near Crouch Hill?

5 How is the distinctive street pattern just north of Endymion Road colloquially known?

6 Lordship Park, in Tottenham just north of this route, is home to what unusual recreation area? Which government department opened the park, in 1938, to teach children about what?

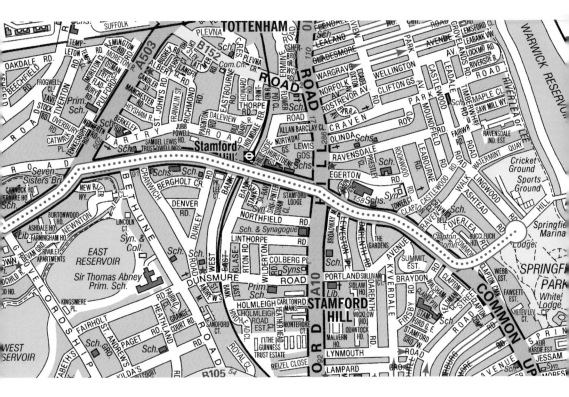

7 The Georgian Orthodox Cathedral Church of the Nativity of Our Lord is opposite a synagogue in which road just off Clapton Common? An unusual church with one of London's most extravagant exteriors, it was built in the nineteenth century as a home for which religious sect that took its name from the Greek for 'abode of love'?

8 Towards the end of the twentieth century Clapton's high crime rate earned it what unenviable nickname?

9 Where near this route were there once three country houses standing in their estates, one of which still stands? What is the name of the remaining house?

The metered taxi fare is the maximum a driver is legally allowed to ask for the journey – hence, in the trade, the slang for not tipping is 'going legal' or being 'legalled off'. Someone who doesn't pay at all is known as a 'bilker'.

Bilkers are sometimes quite creative – reports a few years ago told of one unfortunate taxi driver who took a group of punters home to separate destinations. When he got to the final address, he discovered to his great fury and financial misfortune that what he'd been told was a drunkenly slumbering female passenger who would pay, was in fact a fully dressed and bewigged mannequin.

One reason for the London taxi being so spacious inside is that archaic regulations stated a gentleman should be able to board and sit comfortably inside the vehicle without removing his bowler hat.

03

Primrose Hill Road, NW3 to Donnington Road, NW10

Leave by Adelaide Road, forward Hillgrove Road, comply roundabout, leave by Belsize Road, right Abbey Road, forward West End Lane, left Quex Road, right Kilburn High Road, left Willesden Lane, left Coverdale Road, right Brondesbury Park, left Sidmouth Road, left Chamberlayne Road, right into Donnington Road

1 Cecil Sharp House in Regent's Park Road, which runs through the heart of Primrose Hill, is the home of what society?

2 The 1678 discovery on Primrose Hill, of the body of MP Sir Edmund Berry Godfrey, murdered with his own sword, was the catalyst for which infamous conspiracy theory? Who was its ringleader?

3 Which playwright has published several volumes of diaries recording the minutiae of his life in and around Primrose Hill, and at his earlier address in nearby Gloucester Crescent? The latter featured in a 2015 film of one of his plays, starring Dame Maggie Smith. What's the name of the film (and the play), and of Maggie Smith's character?

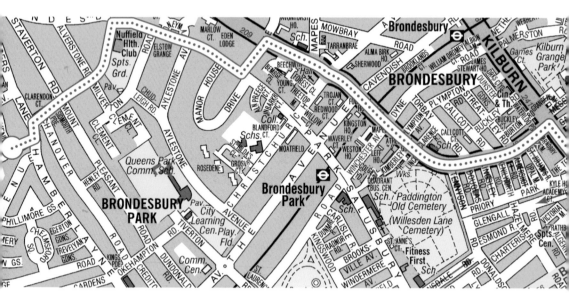

4 Primrose Hill once belonged to which educational institution? Its association with the area lives on in the name of the street in which you'll find the Hampstead what?

5 Which building, founded 1134, stood at what is now the western end of Belsize Road? At the time, a Roman road crossed a river at this point. What was the name of the river and the road?

6 What surprising misfortune befell Kilburn pub the Carlton Arms in April 2015, and what was Westminster Council's surprising response to it?

7 An award-winning 2000 Zadie Smith novel is set in which area on this route? What is the name of the novel?

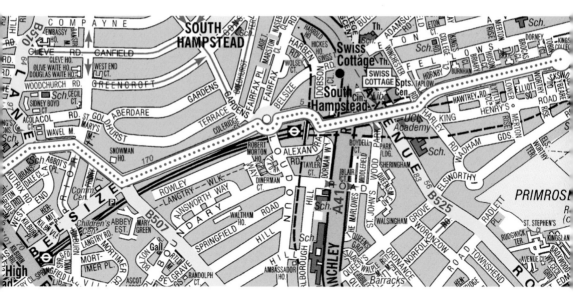

8 Where, near this route, was locally popular (if somewhat prosaic) graffiti quoting the Blur lyric, 'And the view's so nice' replaced by a monument inscribed with, 'I have seen the spiritual sun'? The latter is a quote from which poet? The former is from which song?

9 About which place near this route did William Blake write, '[it] is the mouth of the Furnace & the Iron Door'? In which poem?

10 Which area on this route takes its name from a nineteenth-century pub? What is the name of the pub trading on the site now?

04

Golborne Road, W10 to Pennine Drive, NW2

Leave by Elkstone Road, left Great Western Road, forward Elgin Avenue, left Chippenham Road, left Shirland Road, right Fernhead Road, left Kilburn Lane, right Premier Corner, left Salusbury Road, forward Brondesbury Park, right The Avenue, forward Cavendish Road, left Shoot Up Hill, right Mill Lane, left Fordwych Road, right Minster Road, left Westbere Road, forward Lichfield Road, forward Claremont Road, right into Pennine Drive

1   The streets of North Kensington, around Golborne Road, were the scene of what in 1958, which led to the first what in 1959?

2   Which iconic brutalist tower block stands in Golborne Road, and who designed it?

3   Which street near the start of this route was renamed after a British naval victory in 1739, against the Spanish in the Gulf of Mexico? What was the unusual name of the war? The street now claims to house the world's largest what?

4 Kensal Green is home to one of London's 'Magnificent Seven' what? Which titan of the Victorian era is connected with it, and how? His legacy lives on in which two features on the map at the beginning of this route?

5 Which columnist, humourist and broadcaster who died in 2007 was sometimes called the 'Sage of Cricklewood', after the area in which he lived and which featured in much of his writing? What are the names of his two children, both of whom have forged similar careers?

6 Which semi-professional football team played its home games at Claremont Road from 1926 until 2008?

7 What do the street names in the estate at the end of this route all have in common, and what is the name of the estate? Which Hollywood film star grew up here? In a 1955 film she played an inner-city missionary alongside Marlon Brando and Frank Sinatra. What was the name of the film, and her role in it?

8 '[A]n heroically isolated fragment of the modern city London might once have become [. . .] like Angkor Wat, [it] is a stone dream that will never awake.' Which author wrote these words about which road near this route?

9 This route took you through five London boroughs. Which five?

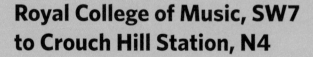

05

Royal College of Music, SW7 to Crouch Hill Station, N4

Leave on the right Prince Consort Road, left Exhibition Road, forward Alexandra Gate, forward West Carriage Drive, forward Serpentine Bridge, forward Serpentine Road, forward West Carriage Drive, forward Victoria Gate, left Bayswater Road, right Lancaster Terrace, left and right Sussex Gardens, forward Old Marylebone Road, right Marylebone Road, left York Gate, forward York Bridge, right Inner Circle, right Chester Road, left Outer Circle, right Gloucester Gate, forward Parkway, forward Britannia Junction, leave by Camden Road, forward Parkhurst Road, forward Seven Sisters Road, left Hornsey Road, right Hanley Road, left Crouch Hill, set down on the right

1 Who was the Prince Consort? Which three attractions near the start of this route are named after him? How does the name of Exhibition Road also relate to him? And what alternative name for the area around Exhibition Road, nowadays largely forgotten, also pays tribute to him?

2 On your right as you enter Hyde Park you can see two iconic London landmarks, around 5 and 8 km (3 and 5 miles) away. What are they?

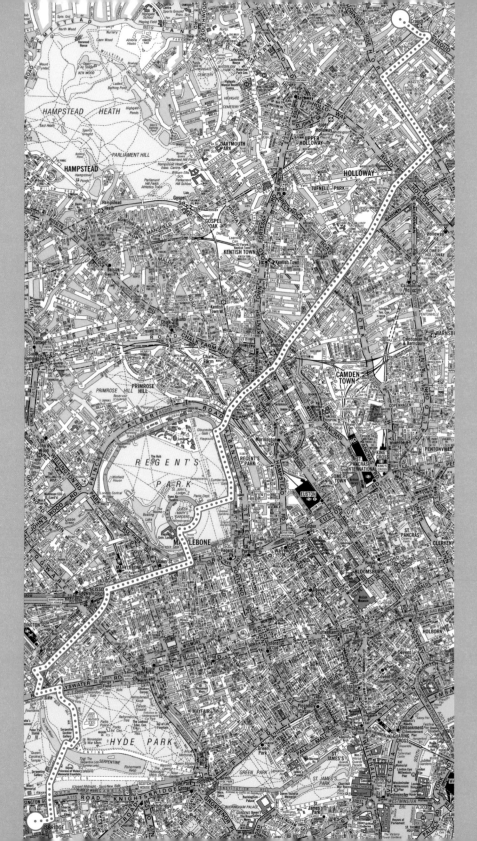

3 Organisers pulled the plug on a megastar's set in Hyde Park in summer 2012. Which megastar and why?

4 Regent's Park was redeveloped and renamed in the early nineteenth century as the northern end of a grand thoroughfare leading south through the West End to whose mansion, overlooking St James's Park and recalled in the name of which modern street? Who was the architect that masterminded this plan? What was Regent's Park called originally?

5 Which British film – partly set in nearby Camden Town – closes with an out-of-work actor performing a Shakespeare soliloquy in the rain in Regent's Park? Which Shakespeare play is he quoting from? And why are wolves wandering around behind him?

6 A short distance south of Parkway is a residential street famous for decades to Radio 4 listeners. Why? What's the name of the street?

7 Who made his last stage appearance at the Electric Ballroom, Camden High Street, in August 1978?

8 What were the 'seven sisters' from which Seven Sisters Road takes its name?

9 Which football team plays its home games a ball's kick from here, and where did it originally play? What derogatory nickname is sometimes used to refer to their ground, and why?

10 A little further north, Holloway Road becomes Archway Road on the hill leading up towards Highgate, with spectacular views of the City. What is this spot's connection with theatre and medieval politics? And from which arch does Archway take its name?

06

Woodsford Square, W14
to Chiswick Mall, W6

Leave on the right Addison Road, forward Holland Park Gardens, left Holland Park Avenue, comply Holland Park roundabout, leave by Shepherd's Bush Green, left Shepherd's Bush Road, left Hammersmith Broadway, right Butterwick, right Talgarth Road, right Queen Caroline Street, left Hammersmith Bridge Road, bear right Great West Road, left South Black Lion Lane, right into Chiswick Mall

1 Just south of Woodsford Square, Melbury Road has, in recent years, been the scene of a public spat between two famous neighbours over a much-wrangled extension application. One, an elder statesman of British rock, has obstructed the plans of the younger star next door to build a basement swimming pool, fearing the excavations will damage his Grade-I listed mansion. The latter has reportedly responded by 'blasting Black Sabbath'. Which two stars?

2 At which building, standing in a street just west of Shepherd's Bush Green until it was demolished in 1993, did the BBC shoot countless television programmes between 1950 and 1991? Which music venue on the west side of the Green and still functioning today, was the BBC Television Theatre throughout most of the same period? And on what street nearby did BBC Television have its headquarters from 1960 to 2013?

3 Which football team has played most of its home games in the last century near Shepherd's Bush Green? What is the ground called? What other nearby stadium – demolished in 1985 – housed the same team briefly in the early 1930s and again in the early 1960s? In what year did this stadium open, and for what purpose?

4 What is the hospital in Hammersmith called? Why? And where is Hammersmith Hospital?

5 Which public house at 19 Upper Mall, Hammersmith, is in the *Guinness Book of Records* for what distinction? Despite this, it is a popular spot for fans of which sporting event? And in connection with that, what did Trenton Oldfield do just upriver from here in 2012?

6 Which artist, designer, writer, publisher and early socialist lived in a house in Upper Mall, just downriver from Chiswick Mall, until his death in 1896? Previous occupant Sir Francis Ronalds, commemorated by a plaque on the building, used the garden to construct the first what – using 13 km (8 miles) of iron wire – in 1816?

7 Which famous London product – named after the city – is manufactured on Chiswick Mall? Who produces it?

8 Which street on this route is named after a co-founder of *The Spectator* magazine? In which nearby mansion did he live until his death in 1719?

9 Which place name near this route traces its not-so-ancient derivation back to a patch of Australian farmland?

07

→

Ravenscourt Park, W6
to Gwendolen Avenue, SW15

Leave on the left King Street, left Studland Street, right Glenthorne Road, bear right Beadon Road, forward Hammersmith Broadway, right Butterwick, right Talgarth Road, left Fulham Palace Road, comply roundabout, leave by Fulham High Street, right Putney Bridge Approach, forward Putney Bridge, forward Putney High Street, forward Putney Hill, right St John's Avenue, left or right into Gwendolen Avenue

1   Ravenscourt Park was created from the grounds of which manor house, commemorated in the name of a nearby road? Why, when he moved in in the eighteenth century, did Thomas Corbett rename the building Ravenscourt House?

2   Across the river from the Fulham Palace Road area, reservoirs from which waterworks – whose name lives on in that of several local features – have been converted into what? Peter Scott, the founder of which organisation that runs it, also designed what iconic logo? Who was his more famous father?

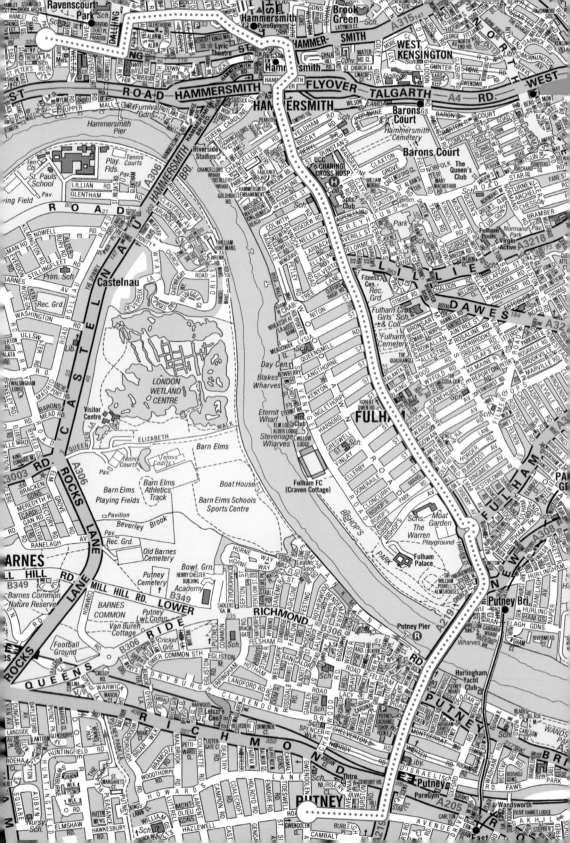

3 Which restaurant overlooks the River Thames in Rainville Road, just south of Hammersmith? Which famous London architect, who is connected to the restaurant in what other way, oversaw its conversion from industrial premises in 1987?

4 What is the nickname of Fulham FC? How did their ground get its name? What street is it on?

5 Fulham Palace was for more than a thousand years until 1973 the residence of the holder of which office? Many non-native species of what were first introduced to the United Kingdom here in the sixteenth to eighteenth centuries?

6 Which club, just east of Putney Bridge Station, was the site of the first match in which sport, in 1874?

7 Putney Bridge is unique among London's River Thames bridges in that it still has what at both ends, historically a common sight at river crossings generally?

8 A Booker-prize-winning historical novel opens with a blacksmith's son receiving a violent beating from his father in Putney. What is the son's name, and that of the novel?

9 Which nineteenth-century novelist has a street named after him off Putney High Street?

10 St Mary's Church, Putney, houses an exhibition on what event that took place here in 1647? What is this event's connection with the brewer's son in question 8?

08

Wimbledon Park Road, SW19 to Plough Road, SW11

Leave by Replingham Road, left Merton Road, right Kimber Road, forward Swaffield Road, right St Ann's Hill, left Earlsfield Road, forward Windmill Road, forward Spencer Park, right North Side Wandsworth Common, forward Battersea Rise, left Bolingbroke Grove, forward Strath Terrace, forward into Plough Road

1 Heading south, what does Wimbledon Park Road's name become? Which private members' club has its address here?

2 Just west of Wimbledon Park Road is London's oldest what? In which street did it open in 1926?

3 At 172 Trinity Road, just south of the junction with Windmill Road, a blue plaque marks the nineteenth-century home of which novelist, who is connected in what way to a churchyard in King's Cross? Which prime minister lived across the road at 191 between 1900 and 1904?

4 Where is the windmill after which Windmill Road is named?

5 The site of which 1988 disaster is marked by a memorial in Spencer Park?

6 What is the name of the River Thames tributary that flows through – and is named after – Wandsworth? A company named Sambrook's based just north of the end of this route manufactures what product, named after this river?

7 Which street on this route is named after a convicted murderer?

8 Which institution near this route was co-founded by Elizabeth I?

9 Which street near this route has been home to both Oscar Wilde and Julian Assange?

There are nine remaining windmills in the Greater London area – the one in Plumstead Common is now part of the Old Mill pub.

The London Taxi Drivers Children's Charity has been taking underprivileged children on annual seaside outings – by cab – since 1931. The first trip was organised by cabbie Mick Cohen, who had himself grown up in the Norwood orphanage they set out from.

09

Streatham Place, SW2 to Waldram Park Road, SE23

Leave by Christchurch Road, left Hardel Rise, right Tulse Hill, forward Thurlow Park Road, forward Dulwich Common, right Lordship Lane, forward London Road, left Devonshire Road, right Waldram Crescent, left into Waldram Park Road

1   A blue plaque at 3 Court Lane Gardens in Dulwich marks the birthplace of which heroine of London adventurers, born in 1906?

2   Dulwich is home to London's oldest what? What is its name? London's last operational what is in College Road?

3   Dulwich Village's streetscape is notable for what quintessentially suburban feature, more usually associated with Middle America than South London?

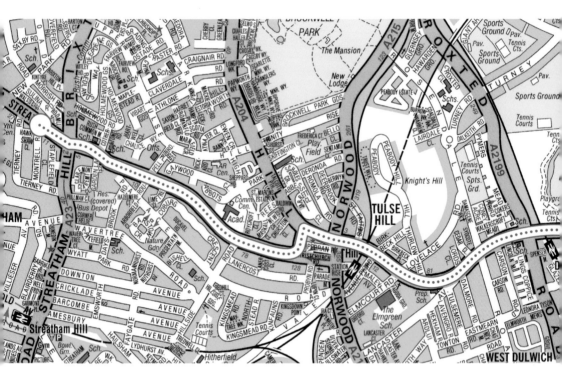

4 In London Road, the Horniman Museum's most popular exhibit is what unconvincingly stuffed creature? How did it happen to be so unconvincingly stuffed? And how did Frederick John Horniman, the Victorian businessman and philanthropist who founded the museum, make his money?

5 Honor Oak Road, off London Road, is named after a tree beneath which who is said to have dined and rested on a journey to Lewisham in 1602?

6 Local band Carter the Unstoppable Sex Machine wrote the lines, 'from the brothels of Streatham / to the taking of Peckham / fun, fun, fun / Here we come!'. Where, on this route, were they writing about? Their song title punned that of a rather more famous one by Gene Pitney. Name both songs.

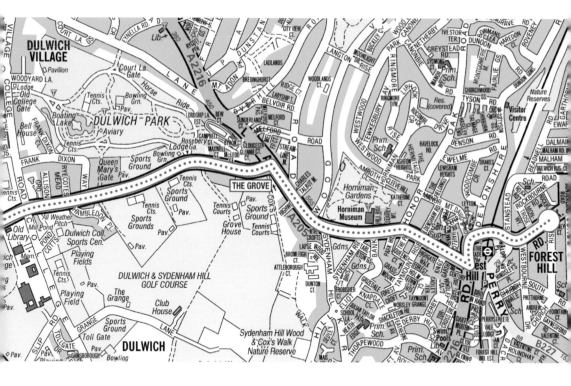

7 The lake in a park near this route is the only surface stretch of a River Thames tributary. What's the name of the park and the river?

8 Which institution on this route was founded by an Elizabethan actor? What was his name, which lives on in that of nearby streets? In this context, what do Brexit Party leader Nigel Farage and Green Party co-leader Jonathan Bartley have in common? And if you added legendary entertainer and comedian Bob Monkhouse to the list, why would he be the odd one out?

9 What do all the streets on this route have in common?

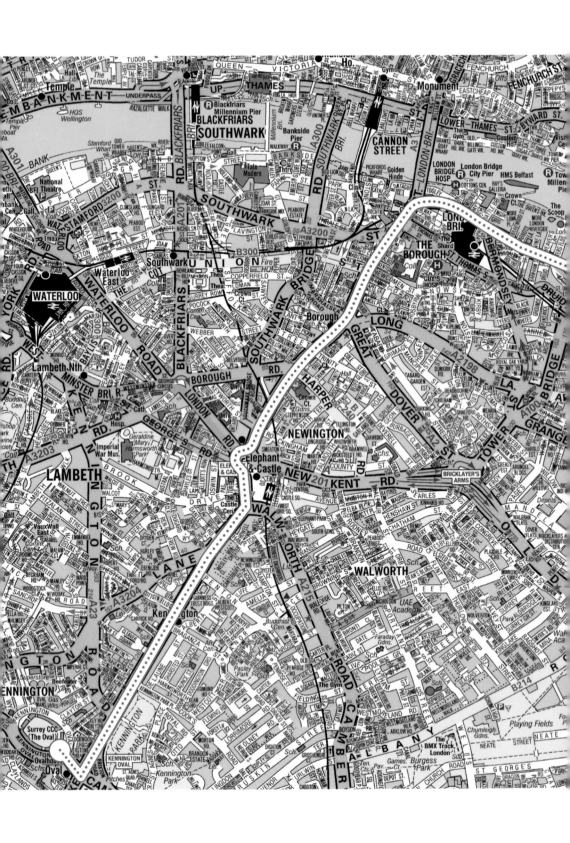

10

Shadwell Station, E1 to The Oval, SE11

Leave on the right Cable Street, left Dock Street, right East Smithfield, left Tower Bridge Approach, forward Tower Bridge, forward Tower Bridge Road, right Tooley Street, forward Duke Street Hill, left Borough High Street, forward Newington Causeway, comply Elephant and Castle, leave by Newington Butts, forward Kennington Park Road, right Harleyford Street, right Kennington Oval, set down on the left

A newly qualified taxi driver is known in the trade as a 'butter boy' or 'butter girl'. No-one seems to be quite sure where this comes from, but it's thought to be from either the idea that new drivers who don't know the trade's intricate etiquette are slippery and not to be trusted; that they take the bread and butter from the mouths of established drivers and their families; or simply a corruption of 'but a boy', in reference to their youthful naivety.

1 Cable Street was named after what, and why?

2 Just south of the western end of Cable Street in tiny Graces Alley, Wilton's is the country's oldest surviving what? Buildings on this site have served more or less the same purpose since 1690. For a period between 1888 and 1956, however, the building was used for something else. What was it?

3 What is the saintly connection between Tooley Street, a hospital near this route and the king of Norway between 1015 and 1028?

4 Which two London Underground lines run through London Bridge Station? Which of them had a last-minute name change in the late 1970s and why? What was its name originally intended to be?

5 An independent museum in Dugard Way, just off Newington Butts, is devoted to the history of which art form? It is sited in a building that once served as what? Who – fittingly – is believed to have lived here, briefly, as a nine-year-old, in 1896?

6 Which pub, demolished in the 1960s, stood at the junction of Kennington Road and Kennington Park Road? What pivotal event happened here in 1845, relating to the history of which building nearby?

7 On 5th March 1870, The Oval hosted the world's first international match in which sport, between which two teams?

8 Which battle took place on this route on 4th October 1936, and who fought it?

9 Where on this route would you have found a shallow spring in the Middle Ages?

10 Which street near this route did Charles Dickens describe as a 'reservoir of dirt, drunkenness and drabs'? By what name was it known in Dickens' time? Which shocking events took place here in December 1811?

11 The design of which building close to this route was intended by its architect to recall the sails of ships moored in the River Thames? Who was the architect?

'Following the cotton' in the taxi trade means going the right way. It comes from the old practice of Knowledge students sticking pins in a map and stringing a piece of cotton between them. The best route was the one that stayed as close to the cotton as possible.

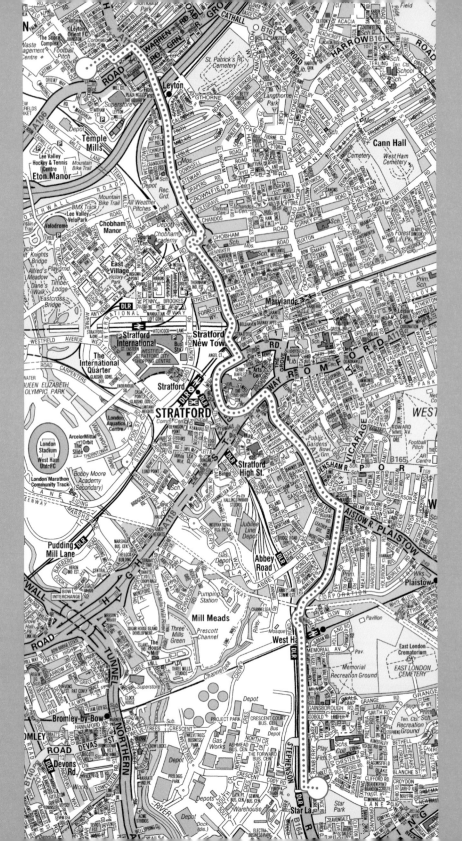

11

Star Lane, E16
to Oliver Road, E10

Leave on the right Manor Road, left New Plaistow Road, forward West Ham Lane, forward Tramway Avenue, left Broadway, right Great Eastern Road, left Angel Lane, forward Leyton Road, comply roundabout, leave by Chobham Road, left Major Road, forward Leyton High Road, left Adelaide Road, right York Road, left Dunedin Road, left or right into Oliver Road

1   Jack Warner, who played the titular character in a classic TV series, is among many notable figures buried near the start of this route. What was the name of the TV show, and of the burial ground? Also buried here is Carl Hans Lody. In 1914, he became the first person in 167 years to have what happen to him, where, and why?

2   Stratford takes its name from a Roman ford over which river? Which other district on this route takes its name from the same river?

3 As you drive up Angel Lane, the UK's fourth largest what looms on your left. What is its name? And what are the top three?

4 Beyond that, lies which park, opened in what year? Which football team now plays its home games here, and what is the stadium called? What is filmmaker Danny Boyle's connection with it? And where was the team's previous stadium?

5 One of Leyton's notable historic residents was Harry Beck, creator of which ubiquitous piece of London design?

6 You end your journey adjacent to the home ground of which football club? What is their ground called? What is their nickname?

7 Where near this route are you likely to bump into confused Beatles fans?

8 Which building near this route was designed by an award-winning British-Iraqi architect who died in 2016? What was her name?

9 In an unusual inversion, an area just off this route takes its name from another country that more commonly has place names taken from the UK. Which area, and why is it so called?

12

Copenhagen Street, N1
to Charing Cross Station, WC2

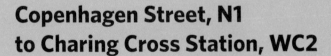

Leave by Caledonian Road, forward King's Cross Bridge, right Grays Inn Road, forward Euston Road, left Upper Woburn Place, forward Tavistock Square, forward Woburn Place, forward Russell Square, forward Southampton Row, forward Kingsway, right Great Queen Street, forward Long Acre, left Bow Street, forward Wellington Street, right Exeter Street, right Strand, left into station forecourt, set down on the left

1 On your left at the bottom of Caledonian Road is one of the area's tiniest and most unusual streets. It is said to be the what, with the tightest what, in Europe? Why does this give it something in common with the London taxi? What is this street called? Historically the area around King's Cross was synonymous with drug dealing and prostitution, a consequence of which was that this hidden away little street was also one of the first in the country to be installed with what?

2 On your right in Woburn Place is London's largest what? What does it boast 1,630 of? What is its name?

3 The Bow Street Runners were London's first what? What is their connection, by a degree or two of separation, with actor Albert Finney?

4   Which seventeenth-century architect designed Covent Garden Piazza, on your right as you drive down Bow Street? Until 1973 it was one of London's great markets – specialising in what? And which celebrated violent misogynist and baby killer's first sighting in England was in Covent Garden in 1662? Who recorded the sighting?

5   The Strand Palace Hotel, the back of which is on your left as you drive down Exeter Street, is on the site of the eighteenth-century Exeter Exchange. Which unusual residents once lived here, many of whom moved to more salubrious accommodation in Regent's Park when the Exchange was demolished in 1829?

6   As you wait at the lights in Exeter Street, to turn right into Strand, a hotel stands directly in front of you and stretches down to the River Thames. What is its name? What is unusual about its forecourt? Which artist painted river scenes from its windows at the turn of the twentieth century? And Harry Craddock, who held which position here, wrote what influential book?

7   Just off this part of Strand is Carting Lane, site of London's only streetlamp still partly powered by what?

8   The forecourt of Charing Cross Station houses a replica of the Eleanor Cross from which the area takes its name. The original stood just south of what is now Trafalgar Square and was erected in the last decade of the thirteenth century to commemorate whom? What, according to urban legend, is her connection with an area around 1.6 km (1 mile) southeast of here?

9   In the 1960s, the destruction of which building on this route was a catalyst for the saving of which other building on this route? The latter underwent major restoration and renovation in the early twenty-first century. Inside is a statue of the poet who led the campaign. Who was he?

Stage 4:

The
Suburbs

01

Heathrow Terminal 1 to RAF Northolt

Leave by Tunnel Road West, comply airport roundabout, leave by Bath Road slip, forward Bath Road, left High Street Harlington, forward Station Road, right North Hyde Road, comply roundabout, leave by The Parkway, forward Ossie Garvin underpass, forward The Parkway, comply Willow Tree roundabout, leave by The Parkway, comply White Hart roundabout, leave by Ruislip Road, forward West End Road, comply Polish War Memorial, leave by West End Road – RAF Northolt is on your left

1 Which terminal was the first to open at Heathrow Airport, in 1995? And which was the last, in 2008?

2 Who was arrested at Heathrow Airport on 8th June 1968, attempting to board a flight to Brussels? For what crime?

3 Which London writer and broadcaster has written of cross-continental walks, starting at his home in South London and walking all the way to boarding at Heathrow Airport, and then from the next airport to his final destination after the flight? In which part of South London does he live?

4 Who used what name for the first time, on the publication of which 1933 memoir, while living and teaching in Church Road, Hayes, just north of North Hyde Road?

5 Who was chairman of Hayes and Harlington District Council 1961–62 and Mayor of Hillingdon 1971–72?

6 A few miles east of Northolt, along the Western Avenue, stands a local landmark once disdained in Pevsner's Architectural Guides as 'perhaps the most offensive of the modernist atrocities along this road of typical by-pass factories'. Now one of London's most cherished examples of which architectural style, it was built in 1932 to house a factory and offices for which manufacturer?

7 Which bird sits atop the Polish War Memorial, and why?

8 RAF Northolt was the site of the repatriation of whom, in 1997? And whose personal aircraft was housed here from 1944?

9 The name of which area near this route is believed to derive from the Old English for leaping across a river? Which river, which in turn takes its name from which suburb a few miles north of Northolt, whose own name comes from the Old English for a pointed, flat-topped hill?

02

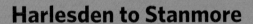

Harlesden to Stanmore

Leave by Craven Park Road, forward Craven Park, forward Hillside, forward Harrow Road, forward High Road, forward Harrow Road, comply roundabout, leave by Harrow Road, comply roundabout, leave by Watford Road, comply roundabout, leave by Sheepcote Road, forward Station Road, forward Railway Approach, forward The Bridge, forward George Gange Way, comply roundabout, leave by George Gange Way, forward High Street, forward High Road, comply roundabout, leave by Uxbridge Road – arrive at Stanmore

1 Which Edinburgh firm opened a factory in Harlesden in 1902, and has been sweetening the air nearby ever since?

2 Just up Brentfield Road, which heads north where Craven Park becomes Hillside, is the world's largest what, outside of India?

··

3 Neasden, just east of Wembley, doesn't have a police station, yet Neasden Police Station appears frequently in the UK print media. Why?

4 Tokyngton Recreation Ground, just south of Wembley Stadium, is home to which relic of football past?

5 Who had the honour of playing the first football match at the new Wembley Stadium in 2007? During excavations to build the stadium, workers removed the foundations of an uncompleted structure that had been intended, in the late nineteenth century, to put Wembley on the map by rivalling what?

6 Local landowner John Lyon, buried at St Mary's Church, Harrow on the Hill, founded which institution? He also left a trust for the upkeep of Edgware Road and which other major road near here? The John Lyon's Charity distributes his estate's largesse among youth projects in seven London boroughs: Barnet, Brent, Camden, Ealing, Hammersmith and Fulham, Harrow, and Kensington and Chelsea. Why those seven boroughs specifically?

7 Also buried at St Mary's Church is Thomas Port, who died in 1838 and lays claim to what unfortunate first? By strange coincidence, a short distance from the church, a plaque marks the site of what other unfortunate first, in 1899?

8 A plaque in London Road, Stanmore, marks the family home of which UK prime minister?

03

East Finchley to Hadley Wood

Leave by North Finchley High Road, left Kingsway, right Ballards Lane, forward Tally Ho Corner, forward Whetstone High Road, forward High Road, forward Great North Road, forward Barnet Hill, forward High Street Barnet, right Hadley Green Road, left Camlet Way, arrive at Hadley Wood

. . . .

1 Who was the MP for Finchley from 1959 until retiring the seat in 1992? Five years later, during election night in 1997, perhaps the most sensational result was the toppling of who by whom, in which neighbouring constituency?

2 What gives Finchley its name?

3 Just off Whetstone High Road, what was the original name of Totteridge & Whetstone Underground station when it opened in 1872?

4 Which event of national significance occurred near what is now called Hadley Green in April 1417? Who stayed in a cottage here, now bearing his name, before exploring the River Zambezi in 1864?

5 A place name on this route suggests it started out as a clearing that was burned from a forest. What is it?

6 What has happened near this route annually or twice annually, more or less every year in one form or another since Elizabethan times? How has it entered the English language?

7 Two London Underground lines terminate on, or near, the northern end of this route. Name the two lines and their respective terminal stations.

8 This route skirts the western edge of an ancient royal hunting ground. What was it called?

04

Lea Bridge to Chingford

Leave by Lea Bridge Road, left Hoe Street, forward Chingford Road, comply Crooked Billet roundabout, leave by Chingford Road, forward Chingford Mount Road, forward Old Church Road, comply roundabout, leave by The Ridgeway – arrive at Chingford

1   What is Walthamstow's postcode, and what's it got to do with Christmas 1994?

2   Whose Walthamstow family home, in Lloyd Park, is now the only public gallery dedicated to his work? Where in Walthamstow are his words, 'Fellowship is life and the lack of fellowship is death' carved in stone?

3   In 2017 actor Paul McGann unveiled a plaque in Walthamstow's Wood Street to mark the site of which building – the first of four in the area – that opened in 1910?

4   What was demolished in the late 1980s to make way for the Crooked Billet roundabout?

5   How old is the church in Old Church Road? Which two East Enders are probably the churchyard's most famous residents?

6   Chingford Plain is home to a hunting lodge named after whom? Who had the lodge built in the 1540s? It stands on the southwestern edge of which Site of Special Scientific Interest?

7   What is the historical importance of the line of sight between Chingford's Pole Hill and Greenwich?

8   Where on this route are strangers welcome?

05

London City Airport to Hornchurch

Leave by Hartman Road, right Connaught Road, comply roundabout, leave by Connaught Road, comply Airport roundabout, leave by Connaught Bridge, comply Connaught roundabout, leave by Royal Albert Way, comply Royal Albert roundabout, leave by Royal Albert Way, comply Beckton Park roundabout, leave by Royal Albert Way, comply Cyprus roundabout, leave by Royal Albert Way, comply Gallions roundabout, leave by Royal Docks Road, comply roundabout, leave by Alfreds Way, forward Lodge Avenue Flyover, forward Ripple Road, bear left slip, comply roundabout, leave by Ripple Road, forward New Road, left Ballards Road, comply Bull roundabout, leave by Rainham Road South, forward Dagenham Road, comply Newtons Corner, leave by Rainham Road, right Ford Lane, left South End Road, right Airfield Way, forward Suttons Lane, forward Station Lane – arrive at Hornchurch

1 Why, along with aviation fuel, does the scent of sugar sometimes linger in the air around London City Airport?

2 East of Royal Docks Road, the old Beckton Gas Works doubled as where, in which 1987 film, directed by whom? The area is named after Simon Adams Beck. Who was he?

3 East of that, covering 100 hectares (250 acres) between Alfreds Way and the River Thames, is Europe's largest what?

4 In September 1878, this stretch of the River Thames saw the largest loss of life in peacetime Britain when which paddle steamer collided with a coal boat? More than six hundred people died, and not all of them by drowning. How is this connected to the answer to question 3?

5 North of Ripple Road, Becontree is home to the UK's largest what? Begun in 1921, what was its primary purpose? Which couple, as recorded on a plaque outside 20 Bushgrove Road, took tea and planted two trees here in 1923?

6 In the 1950s, fifty thousand people were employed where, in Dagenham?

7 For centuries until 1854, Ferry Lane, leading down to the River Thames south of Rainham, was the northern boarding point for a ferry that crossed the river, primarily for what purpose?

8 Just downriver from Rainham, which road crosses the River Thames at the Dartford Crossing?

9 What unique fixture can be seen at the east end of St Andrew's Church roof, Hornchurch, where you might usually expect to find a cross?

It's not as rare
as you might expect
for passengers engaged
in polite conversation to ask
their taxi driver what they do for
a living – on long, late-night
journeys, sometimes
more than once.

London City Airport
opened in 1987 to provide
closer access for smaller planes to
the financial centres in the City and the
newly developed Isle of Dogs, than that
previously offered by suburban Heathrow
and the satellite airports at Gatwick, Luton
and Stansted. It stands on a quay between
the old King George V and Royal Albert
docks, allowing for spectacular,
steep take-offs and landings.

Wherrymen, who ferried passengers across or along
the River Thames, were London's prototype taxi drivers.
They had already been operating for centuries when they
were first regulated by Henry VIII in 1514. Famed for
their bawdy behaviour, their shouts of 'oars' or 'sculls'
advertised their business on the riverbanks.
Their numbers rapidly declined with the
bridge-building initiatives of the eighteenth
and nineteenth centuries.

London's longest-serving taxi driver was Alfred Collins, born in Barnet in 1915. He retired in 2007 after seventy years' service, at the age of 92.

The Thames Path National Trail follows the river for 115 km (184 miles) from its source near the village of Kemble in Gloucestershire to Woolwich. The river itself continues its journey out to the North Sea. The end of London's river jurisdiction is marked on the Essex bank by the Crow Stone near Southend and on the Kent bank by the London Stone on the Isle of Grain.

The Taxi Charity for Military Veterans – founded in Fulham in 1948 – annually escorts veterans by taxi to the Netherlands and Normandy, France, for Second World War commemoration events. Veterans are also given free lifts to the Remembrance Day commemorations in Whitehall each November.

06

Greenwich to Erith

Leave by Romney Road, forward Trafalgar Road, forward Woolwich Road, comply Horn Lane roundabout, leave by Woolwich Road, comply roundabout, leave by Woolwich Road, comply roundabout, leave by Woolwich Road, comply roundabout, leave by Woolwich Church Street, forward High Street Woolwich, comply roundabout, leave by High Street Woolwich, comply roundabout, leave by Beresford Road, forward Plumstead Road, forward Plumstead High Street, forward Bostall Hill, forward Woolwich Road, forward Erith Road, forward Fraser Road, left Bexley Road – arrive at Erith

1 Which valley just south of Woolwich Road is a popular spot for observing red robins?

2 During the First World War, 88,000 people were employed where, in Woolwich? The River Thames at Woolwich is enlivened by a structure that was completed in 1982, and a river crossing that has been open since 1889. What are they?

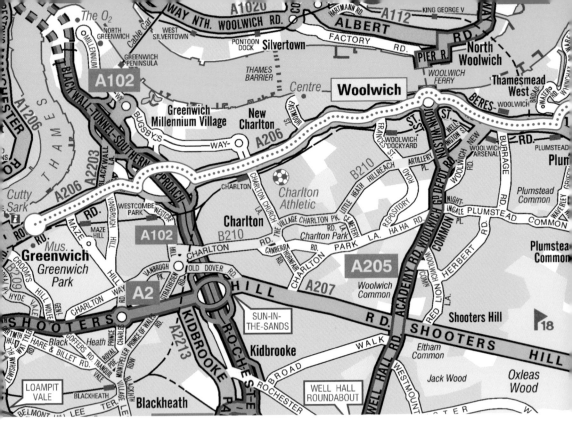

. . . .

3 Woolwich saw the foundation of which first, in 1847, and the opening of which other first, in 1974?

4 Much of which 1971 film, by which director, was filmed among the modernist tower blocks and artificial lakes of Thamesmead, north of Bostall Hill? And what connection do former politicians Jonathan Aitken and Jeffrey Archer share with Thamesmead?

5 When was Thamesmead developed? What was here before then?

6 Erith is home to Greater London's longest what? And which future baronet met his future wife in the 1950s, while running the family business here?

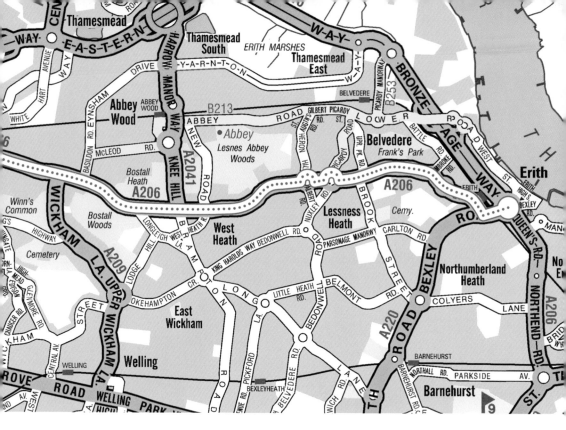

. . . .

7 Southeast of Erith, which ex-pupil of Dartford Grammar School contributed to the founding of a performance venue at the school that bears his name?

8 Southwest of Erith, the Red Barn pub in Barnehurst was at the centre of a post-war revival in what? Who unveiled a plaque at the pub commemorating this in 1985?

9 Talking about her home town, which comedian once said that it 'isn't twinned with anywhere, but it does have a suicide pact with Dagenham'. And what was her home town?

07

Catford to Biggin Hill Airport

Leave by Bromley Road, forward Bromley Hill, forward London Road, left Tweedy Road, forward Kentish Way, forward Masons Hill, forward Bromley Common, comply roundabout, leave by Bromley Common, right Oakley Road, forward Westerham Road, forward Leaves Green Road, forward Main Road – Biggin Hill Airport is on your left

1   Mr Smith's nightclub in 1960s Catford was the setting for a gangland battle, resulting in the death of Kray associate Dickie Hart. The fight was between the Hayward gang and which South London crime family? What consequence followed the next night, and where?

2   Which building, east of Catford and managed by English Heritage, was a medieval and Tudor palace before falling into disrepair and eventually being partially converted into an art deco mansion in the 1930s? What is the building's connection with the Courtauld Gallery in Central London?

3 How is an unassuming terraced house in Plaistow Grove, just east of London Road, connected with a street of 1980s housing called Shannon Way and the bandstand in Croydon Road Recreation Ground, both in nearby Beckenham?

4 Which unusual venue in Chislehurst, east of Bromley, was used as an air-raid shelter during the Second World War and hosted gigs by Jimi Hendrix, Pink Floyd and others in the 1960s?

5 St Mary's Church in Addington, west of Westerham Road, is noted for being the final resting place of several holders of which office, whose country residence was at nearby Addington Palace during the nineteenth century?

6 Part of Biggin Hill Airport is owned by which billionaire business magnate, who keeps a plane here as well as his collection of classic racing cars?

7 '. . . the rebuilt deserts of Central London have nothing like this wholesale transformation of rather staid Victorian lumps into rather shoddy modern boxes . . . potentially a magnificent new city . . .' About which area near this route was architecture critic Ian Nairn writing?

The Worshipful Company of Hackney Carriages is London's 104th livery company. Established in 2004, it carries out charitable works and promotes the taxi trade.

Because of the bend in the River Thames between Westminster and Blackfriars, the most direct routes in London often involve crossing two bridges. In fact, to go from, say, Leadenhall Market in the City to Lower Richmond Road in Putney you could make an argument for three crossings – at London, Lambeth and Putney bridges – but it would probably be a bit extravagant.

The Duke of Edinburgh famously used his own private London taxi – a Metrocab, also used in the trade but not the usual iconic black cab – to get around the city unnoticed. It is now on display in the Royal Garages at Sandringham.

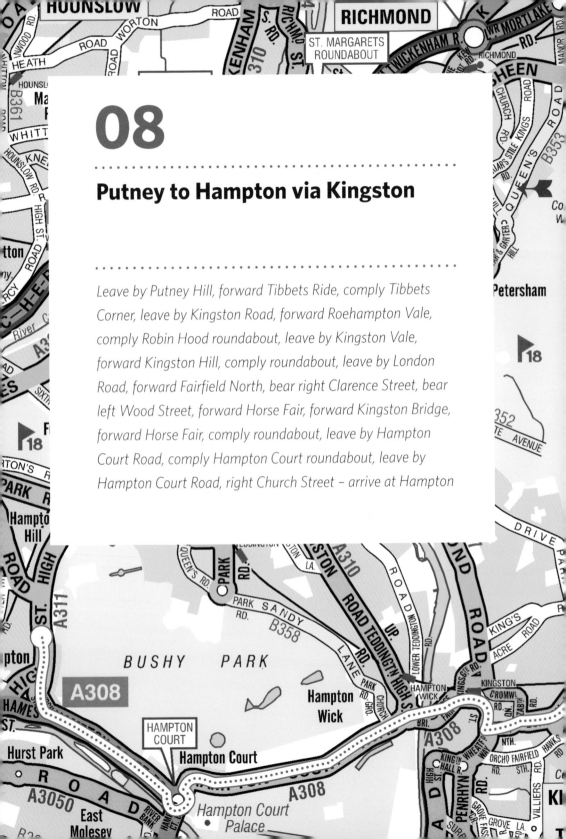

08

Putney to Hampton via Kingston

Leave by Putney Hill, forward Tibbets Ride, comply Tibbets Corner, leave by Kingston Road, forward Roehampton Vale, comply Robin Hood roundabout, leave by Kingston Vale, forward Kingston Hill, comply roundabout, leave by London Road, forward Fairfield North, bear right Clarence Street, bear left Wood Street, forward Horse Fair, forward Kingston Bridge, forward Horse Fair, comply roundabout, leave by Hampton Court Road, comply Hampton Court roundabout, leave by Hampton Court Road, right Church Street – arrive at Hampton

1   Which institution, located north of Roehampton Vale, often appears in the tabloid press, and why? A little northeast, at a bend in the road in Queen's Ride, is a memorial to which musician who died here in 1977?

2   King Henry's Mound in Richmond Park is famous for its protected views of what?

3   Just south of Richmond Park in Kingston, at 2 Liverpool Road, a blue plaque records that Eadweard Muybridge spent his last years here, until his death in 1904. He was a pioneer of which art form, and what did his work tell us about horses? Which twentieth-century painter cited Muybridge's work as invaluable source material?

4   Hampton Court Palace was built in the early 1500s for whom? Who was the last monarch to live here? What sport is still played here, on facilities upgraded by Charles II in the 1660s?

5   Bushy Park, on the north side of Hampton Court Road, was the wartime base of Supreme Headquarters Allied Expeditionary Force. Who was its commander? In a Victorian tradition that was revived in the 1970s, what happens here each year on the Sunday closest to 11th May? And what is Christopher Wren's connection with the event?

6   This route passes through, or by, two of London's eight what? What are their names, and those of the other six?

7   What, near this route, connects a Balkan republic with the largest town on the Scottish island of Mull?

8   A video uploaded to YouTube in November 2011 of whom, doing what, where, near this route, has to date had over 21,000,000 views?

The taxi trade
feeds a large satellite
industry of mechanics, rental
fleets, dedicated recovery vehicles,
advertising livery fitters, insurers and
accountants – not to mention cafes and petrol
stations (or, increasingly, charging points).
Traditionally the East End has been home to
much of this industry. Dunbridge Street and
Three Colts Lane in Bethnal Green still
largely consist of these businesses,
housed in arches under
railway viaducts.

The gardens at Hampton Court
Palace are home to the world's oldest
puzzle maze (dating from around
1700) and the world's largest grape
vine (planted by Capability Brown).

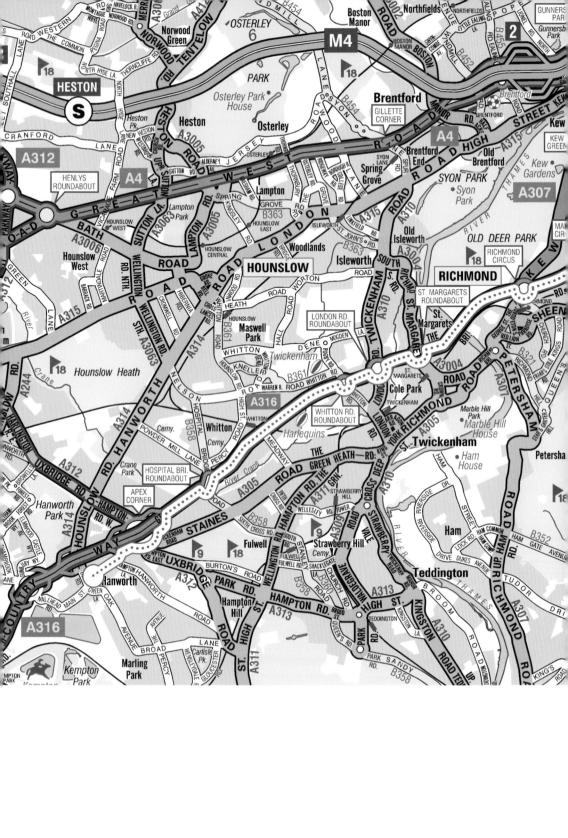

09

Hammersmith to Hanworth

Leave by Hammersmith Bridge Road, right Great West Road, forward Great Chertsey Road, comply Hogarth roundabout, leave by Burlington Lane, forward Alexandra Avenue, forward Great Chertsey Road, forward Chiswick Bridge, forward Clifford Avenue, forward Lower Richmond Road, comply Manor Circus, leave by Lower Mortlake Road, comply Richmond Circus, leave by Twickenham Road, forward Twickenham Bridge, forward The Avenue, comply St Margarets roundabout, leave by Chertsey Road, comply London Road roundabout, leave by Chertsey Road, comply Whitton Road roundabout, leave by Chertsey Road, comply Hospital Bridge roundabout, leave by Great Chertsey Road, bear left slip road, comply Apex Corner, leave by slip road, bear left Swan Road – arrive at Hanworth

1 Who, commemorated in a nearby street name, built and lived in Chiswick House? And who, commemorated in another nearby street name, lived in a house around the corner?

2 A large part of Kew Gardens' early collections consisted of specimens gathered by botanist Sir Joseph Banks on eighteenth-century maritime voyages with whom? Banks also supplied an Eastern Cape giant cycad that is still going strong today and claims which world-beating distinction? The Royal Botanical Gardens at Kew are one of London's four what? Where are the other three?

3 Apart from the Royal Botanical Gardens, which other major historic collection is Kew home to?

4 What is the connection between the Beatles and a building just south of St Margarets roundabout?

5 Where, near Twickenham, famously played host to a series of shows by emerging stars such as the Rolling Stones in the early 1960s? Just upriver from there is a spectacular eighteenth-century villa with an architectural style named after it. Which architectural style, and which house? And which politician and aristocrat built it?

6 Michael O'Brien achieved what first at Twickenham Stadium in 1974?

7 Just south of Twickenham, Teddington marks which point on the River Thames?

8 A correctional facility lies near the end of this route – what is its name and why has Poet Laureate Simon Armitage spent time there?

Kew Palace – the smallest of London's Historic Royal Palaces and a Georgian country retreat – was the scene of much of the 'mad' King George III's secluded treatment. He was subject to the use of emetics, laxatives, freezing baths, leeches and strait-jackets during his regular bouts of illness from 1788, which eventually led to the declaration of the Regency in 1811.

Turning down a fare is known as 'brooming' in the trade, and very much frowned upon by drivers. It's also technically illegal – London taxis are required by the terms of their licenses to accept any job under 19 km (12 miles) in distance or an hour in duration.

One old cabbies' saying goes 'Bermondsey pays better than Belgravia', reflecting the sadly true notion that generosity is more likely to be found among working Londoners than the gentry.

The
Answers

⇥ 56s

Map Test

1 Kings Place; *The Guardian*; Prince
2 The British Library; The Francis Crick Institute
3 University of the Arts London (UAL), or Central St Martins, in Granary Square; it was a grain store
4 Gasholders
5 The Hardy Tree (after the writer, Thomas Hardy); St Pancras Station; St Pancras Old Church
6 Maple Street (at the London Telecom Tower)
7 Thomas Coram; Queen Square and Great Ormond Street
8 Euston Road (The Wellcome Collection)
9 Friends House in Euston Road, home of the Quakers; Stephenson Way, home of the Magic Circle
10 Gower Street (to the Grant Museum of Zoology)

The King's Cross gasholders, a fixture on the local skyline for a century and a half, were removed piece by piece to Yorkshire in the early 2010s. Shepley Engineers Ltd painstakingly restored the gasholders before returning them to King's Cross for re-erection in their current location.

56.1

1 A long-standing coaching house – a tavern stood on the junction of Green Lanes and Seven Sisters Road from the early nineteenth century to the late twentieth century; they all played there in the 1960s
2 East Reservoir and West Reservoir; London Bridge; Castle Climbing Centre
3 Crufts dog show
4 It is Islington's oldest building; Francis Bacon
5 One of the UK's first gay weddings
6 Tony Blair and Gordon Brown – they supposedly made a Labour Party leadership succession pact there on this occasion
7 Lord Liverpool, British Prime Minister 1812–27
8 Joe Orton; Fieldway Crescent, at the junction with Holloway Road
9 Victoria Line
10 Clissold Park

56.2

1 The New River; it is an artificial river built in the seventeenth century to bring fresh water into London from Hertfordshire; Hugh Myddelton MP was instrumental in (and largely funded) its construction
2 A theatre, on the site of a well; Sadler's Wells Theatre
3 The British Postal Museum (at Mount Pleasant Sorting Office)
4 UK Prime Minister, 1894–95
5 Centre Point; homelessness
6 Soho; markets
7 Oasis; *(What's the Story) Morning Glory?*
8 Cholera
9 William Blake

56.3

1 (Madame) Marie Tussaud

2 They are recreating the famous cover photograph for *Abbey Road*, the Beatles' final studio album (1969), which was taken on the pedestrian crossing outside the Abbey Road Studios at which it was recorded, at the southwest end of Abbey Road; Lisson Grove

3 By the first omnibus service, launched 1829, which ran from Paddington Green to the Bank of England

4 The now, mainly buried, River Westbourne, after which the terrace is named; it flows through the Serpentine, is piped over the platforms at Sloane Square and into the Thames at Chelsea Reach

5 *Peter Pan*; JM Barrie (*Peter Pan*'s author)

6 Cardinal John Henry Newman; both men got married here

7 St John's Wood

8 Lord's Cricket Ground

9 Little Venice

56.4

1 Theatre; the London Coliseum

2 The centre of London, for the purpose of measuring distance to London (for example, on motorway signs)

3 The Queen Mother; Prince Charles and Camilla Parker Bowles

4 The Duke of Wellington; No 1 London

5 Department store; Harrods; an escalator

6 House; Buckingham Palace

7 Chelsea FC; Stamford Bridge

8 Knightsbridge

9 Fulham Road; cancer

10 Constitution Hill

56.5

1 £21.6 million; 378 (of the latest TX model at the time, at £57,099)

2 She lived in a house on this site from 1866 to 1913; Brompton Cemetery (from names on the headstones)

3 Bob Dylan

4 Kensington Palace

5 The *Evening Standard*; *Daily Mail*

6 The Design Museum

7 Opera

8 Notting Hill Carnival; Hugh Grant (*Notting Hill*); Portobello Market (Portobello Road)

9 Cromwell Road (named after Richard Cromwell, son of Oliver)

56.6

1 Waterloo Bridge: Napoleon was defeated at the Battle of Waterloo, after which Waterloo Station – and hence the bridge – is named; Abba won the Eurovision Song Contest in 1974 with their breakthrough single, 'Waterloo'; and 'Terry meets Julie, Waterloo Station, every Friday night' are lyrics from the Kinks' 1967 hit single 'Waterloo Sunset'

2 Catherine Street

3 Tottenham Court Road, Oxford Circus and Bond Street; Central Line

4 HMV

5 Harry Gordon Selfridge, owner of Selfridges department store

6 Baker Street; Sherlock Holmes; 221b

7 Marble Arch; it was the site of a notorious public gallows known as the Tyburn Tree

8 It is the London home of ex-Prime Minister Tony Blair

9 Michael Bond (Bond Street); Isambard Kingdom Brunel

56.7

1 Members of Parliament; a portcullis – the portcullis is a symbol of the House of Commons

2 Not the clock tower of the Houses of Parliament (officially the Elizabeth Tower, previously St Stephen's Tower), but the bell inside it

3 The expanding sewage system; Joseph Bazalgette

4 Cleopatra's Needle; two sphinxes lie facing the needle – in ancient Egypt they would have been facing away from it, as its guardians

5 Clock face; the clock face of the Elizabeth Tower ('Big Ben') at the Houses of Parliament

6 The Garden Bridge

7 The River Fleet, a tributary of the River Thames crossed by Fleet Street at present-day Ludgate Circus; newspapers

8 Sweeney Todd ('the demon barber of Fleet Street'); Dr Samuel Johnson; *A Dictionary of the English Language*

9 Barbican Estate

10 Smithfield; meat; Bartholomew Fair (St Bartholomew's Hospital)

11 Charterhouse Street and Charterhouse Square; Hercule Poirot

56.8

1 Cricket

2 John Wesley; Methodism

3 Bunhill Fields Burial Ground; they were all dissenters or nonconformists – the burial ground was established for this purpose

4 Tower 42; the UK's tallest building (183 m/600 ft); it is in the shape of the NatWest logo

5 The moat outside the wall of the Roman city

6 The White Tower, built by William the Conqueror in the 1080s; he was a German spy; Ronald and Reginald Kray; failure to attend National Service

7 Realising the bridge was opening, and it being too late to brake, Gunter slammed his foot on the accelerator and his bus leaped the gap

8 HMS *Belfast*; its guns are trained on the London Gateway services

9 Wormwood Street and Camomile Street

56.9

1 Captain James Cook; Dr Thomas Barnardo

2 *Call the Midwife*

3 Chinese (Chinatown is now in the West End)

4 Regent's Canal

5 The Limehouse Declaration; the 'Gang of Four'; The Social Democratic Party (SDP), which eventually merged with the Liberal Party to become the Liberal Democrats in 1988

6 Isambard Kingdom Brunel (Brunel Road); for fears that horses pulling vehicles would otherwise bolt for the light at the opposite end as soon as they entered the tunnel

7 JMW Turner (*The Fighting Temeraire*, 1838)

8 The Pilgrim Fathers, founders of New England (in the *Mayflower* ship)

9 Greenland Dock

56.10

1 London County Council until 1965, subsequently the Greater London Council; London Dungeon, London Aquarium and Shrek's Adventure

2 The London Eye; Ferris wheel

3 The Festival of Britain, 1951 – a national exhibition for which much of the South Bank complex was built

4 The Oxo Tower in Barge House Street

5 The Millennium Bridge; it opened in 2000 but wobbled disconcertingly; Tate Modern art gallery; Bankside Power Station; neighbours in luxury apartments who complained their privacy was being compromised by tourists on the Tate's new viewing platform

6 The Bank of England's nickname

7 Big Ben; The Liberty Bell

8 Joseph Merrick, nicknamed the Elephant Man

9 Aldgate (derived from Ale Gate)

10 Brick Lane

56.11

1 A handbag

2 *Upstairs, Downstairs*; *Passport to Pimlico*

3 Charles II; a precursor to croquet, the game was called pall-mall – the origin of both street names

4 The BBC World Service

5 St Paul's Cathedral

6 Bethlehem or Bethlem Hospital; the word 'bedlam' is a corruption of its name

7 Kindertransport – the Arrival; Jewish child refugees rescued from the Nazis

8 London Wall

9 Queen Victoria: Victoria Station, Victoria Coach Station, the Queen Victoria Memorial (outside Buckingham Palace), Victoria Street and Victoria Square

56.12

1 The first flying bomb to land in London

2 The Salvation Army; Ronnie Kray

3 Victoria Park; Bishop's Way

4 The Bethnal Green Tube Disaster, in which 173 people died in a crush while trying to shelter from an air raid; it was the largest UK civilian death toll of any single event in the Second World War

5 Ronnie (March 1995), Charlie (April 2000) and Reggie (October 2000) Kray

6 A notorious slum

7 Columbia Road

8 Silicon roundabout; following highways developments, the junction is no longer a roundabout

9 The Eagle; 'Pop Goes the Weasel' ('Up and down the City Road / In and out of the Eagle')

10 They are the longest on the London Underground network; a pub at the junction of Pentonville Road and Islington High Street, the only colour-grouped property named after a building; the Co-operative Bank stands on the site of the pub – at the time manufacturer Waddington's visited to scout locations, it was a tea house in which they are said to have stopped for refreshments, adding Angel, Islington to the board as a result; a plaque inside the bank records the historic association

Arthur Morrison's *A Child of the Jago*, with its brutal depiction of poverty, caused a sensation when published in 1896. The name was used by a clothing boutique founded a stone's throw from the site of the Old Nichol in Great Eastern Street in 2008 (it has since relocated to Charing Cross Road).

➤ 28s

28.1

1　Euston Arch – gateway to the original Euston Station
2　A flood of beer (specifically London Porter) from Meux & Co's Horse Shoe Brewery; Dominion Theatre
3　*Gin Lane* (1751); St Giles (or the St Giles Rookery); St George's (in Bloomsbury Way)
4　Black Prince Road
5　Vincent van Gogh
6　Brixton Windmill (also known as Ashby's Mill)
7　Bertrand Russell; Mick Jagger
8　Restaurants; The Clink is staffed by inmates working towards cookery and hospitality qualifications
9　David Bowie
10　University College London

28.2

1　John Ruskin; Ruskin Park
2　MI6, or the Secret Intelligence Service, employer of James Bond
3　The July 2005 bombings; animals (the Animals in War memorial)
4　Jimi Hendrix (23) and George Frederick Handel (25). The museum was called the Handel House Museum until the Hendrix rooms were opened to the public in 2016, when it was renamed Handel & Hendrix in London; Claridges (named Mivart's until Claridges next door took it over in the 1850s)
5　John Nash; Buckingham Palace; it had been commandeered for an Extinction Rebellion camp
6　The first parking ticket was issued
7　Marylebone was previously known as Tyburnia, after the River Tyburn; it had become associated with the 'Tyburn Tree' – the public execution site at the south end of Edgware Road
8　*24 Hours in A&E*; King's College Hospital in Denmark Hill
9　Camberwell (the Camberwell Beauty)
10　Speaker's Corner, at the northeastern corner of Hyde Park; Reverend Donald Soper was a famous orator there

28.3

1　Labour Party
2　Residents in the apartments at the top of the building complained about the noise; the Carbuncle Cup, awarded to the worst building of the year
3　Blackfriars Monastery; arts and crafts
4　The legal profession; from the Knights Templar who originally owned this land
5　Central Criminal Court; (Lady) Justice; Newgate Prison
6　Inner London Crown Court (Newington Causeway) and Blackfriars Crown Court (Pocock Street)
7　In the nave of St Paul's Cathedral
8　St Andrew-by-the-Wardrobe
9　Sir Christopher Wren's tomb in St Paul's Cathedral (which Wren designed); anti-capitalist protestors occupied St Paul's Churchyard
10　The Black Friars (of Blackfriars Monastery)

28.4

1　Hans Sloane; Belgravia; Sloane Square
2　Chinatown (left) and Soho (right)
3　*Les Misérables*; The Sondheim Theatre; *Les Misérables*
4　Phileas Fogg sets out on his journey from here in Jules Verne's *Around the World in Eighty Days*; Jubilee Line; between Westminster and Green Park
5　St James's Palace
6　Sir Christopher Wren; Chelsea Pensioners (retired soldiers); The RHS Chelsea Flower Show
7　JMW Turner; troops (from the old Chelsea Barracks nearby) to break step, because of the bridge's structural weakness
8　Sir Thomas More
9　Battersea Arts Centre

28.5

1 James Abbott McNeill Whistler; Whistlers Avenue
2 Whitehall Palace and Hampton Court Palace
3 Chelsea Drugstore
4 Sex Boutique; Malcolm McLaren and Vivienne Westwood; the Sex Pistols were managed by Malcolm McLaren
5 Cadogan Hall (as in Cadogan Street, Lane, Square, etc)
6 The piccadill – a type of collar fashionable in the seventeenth century, and from which tailor Robert Baker made his fortune before building his home nearby
7 Queen Elizabeth II
8 *The Sign of Four* by Sir Arthur Conan Doyle and *The Picture of Dorian Gray* by Oscar Wilde
9 The BBC
10 Berkeley Square; 'A Nightingale Sang in Berkeley Square'
11 Regent Street

28.6

1 The first is out-of-town shopping centre, Brent Cross, which opened in 1976; the second is Britain's first motorway, the M1, which opened in 1959 and links the cities of London and Leeds
2 The Golders Green Hippodrome
3 John Keats, who lived in the street now called Keats Grove; 'Ode to a Nightingale'
4 Sigmund Freud; *Benefits Supervisor Sleeping* is the title of a famous painting of South Londoner Sue Tilley, who worked at Charing Cross Job Centre, by Freud's grandson, the artist Lucian Freud
5 Parliament Hill; Guy Fawkes and his 'Gunpowder Plot' associates
6 The UK's last female hanging; Ruth Ellis
7 It is the deepest station on the network (58.5 m/192 ft below street level)
8 Jack Straw's Castle
9 Ken Livingstone (Brent East) and Glenda Jackson

(Hampstead and Highgate, later Hampstead and Kilburn); London Mayor and Oscar-winning actress

28.7

1 She was haranguing looters in the London riots that followed the fatal police shooting of Mark Duggan in Tottenham
2 Elizabeth Fry
3 It was kept because people doubted the new church tower could take the weight of its bells; St John's; Thomas Cromwell; Hilary Mantel (*Wolf Hall*, *Bring Up the Bodies* and *The Mirror and the Light*)
4 Marie Lloyd
5 Albert Square (*Eastenders*) in Walford, after Walford Road
6 Clowns; Joseph Grimaldi
7 London's first bomb of the First World War exploded, dropped from a Zeppelin
8 The pitch at Highbury Stadium (now Highbury Stadium Square), former home of Arsenal FC
9 *London Fields*, Martin Amis; Broadway Market

28.8

1 Marsh (as in Marsh Wall); the London Docks; the finance industry; Wes Anderson
2 Billingsgate Market; it's a wholesale fish market
3 Sets of traffic lights arranged in the shape of a tree (the sculpture is called *Traffic Light Tree*)
4 A 1930s warehouse that stored fruit shipped in from the Canary Islands
5 The SS *Great Eastern*; Isambard Kingdom Brunel
6 Millwall Dock
7 The trains are driverless – children (and adults) like to sit in the front window; Tower Gateway Station
8 William Cubitt; Mayor of London; Thomas and Lewis
9 Hertsmere Road

28.9

1 The 'Match Girls' – female workers at the Bryant & May factory here
2 River Lea; an arched bridge
3 Balfron Tower (Goldfinger) and Robin Hood Gardens (Smithson)
4 Until the opening of the Dartford Crossing it was the easternmost road crossing of the River Thames
5 The first English settlers of America, founders of the Jamestown colony
6 Gas works; the domed roof of the O2 Arena
7 Walk over the domed roof of the O2 Arena
8 Emirates Air Line cable car
9 Diamonds, from the Millennium Dome (now the O2 Arena)

28.10

1 Gary Oldman
2 Goldsmiths College
3 Christopher Marlowe
4 River Ravensbourne
5 *Golden Hinde*; HMS *Endeavour*
6 *Cutty Sark*
7 Placentia Palace; Henry VIII; Sir Christopher Wren
8 Greenwich Park; Zero; Prime Meridian was established at the Royal Observatory; it is a timepiece introduced in the nineteenth century for ships moored in the River Thames – the ball drops from the top of its pole to the bottom at precisely 1 pm each day
9 Lord Nelson, at the Battle of Trafalgar

28.11

1 Peckham Spring
2 The Shard
3 It's the only property south of the River Thames; Watling Street
4 Charlie Chaplin; Michael Caine

5 It is the home of Ministry of Sound nightclub
6 Imperial War Museum; Pope John Paul II visited during the first-ever visit of a Pope to the United Kingdom
7 The Cenotaph; the laying of the wreaths on Remembrance Day; Sir Edwin Lutyens
8 The cellars of Whitehall Palace, most of which was destroyed by fire at the end of the seventeenth century, are situated beneath it
9 William Wordsworth, about standing on Westminster Bridge (in the poem 'Composed upon Westminster Bridge, September 3, 1802')

28.12

1 Shakespeare's (Globe Theatre); Bear Gardens (bear baiting)
2 Sir Christopher Wren, who was able to observe the construction of his masterpiece St Paul's Cathedral across the river; the plaque is incorrect – Wren lived a few doors down, but when his house was demolished the plaque was rescued and re-sited
3 Westminster Bridge; left-hand driving; it was sold to American Robert P McCulloch and rebuilt in Arizona
4 Walkie-Talkie; its concave glass exterior reflected and intensified the rays of the sun, melting the dashboards of cars parked nearby
5 The A10, Ermine Street, York
6 Daniel Defoe
7 Hasidic Jews
8 Shacklewell
9 Catherine Booth was the 'Mother of the Salvation Army'; her husband, William, was its founder; Abney Park Cemetery stands in the grounds of the old Abney House
10 Their decapitated heads (along with those of countless others) were all displayed on pikes on London Bridge after their execution

→21s

21.1

1 Lord Byron's

2 Writers Karl Marx and Douglas Adams are both buried at Highgate Cemetery, in Swain's Lane; the former was co-author of *Manifesto of the Communist Party*, and the latter wrote the *Hitchhiker's Guide to the Galaxy* series, which features a character called Hotblack Desiato, named after a North London estate agent; William Foyle, co-founder of Foyles bookshop in Charing Cross Road, is also buried here

3 It is outside the home of singer-songwriter George Michael, who died on Christmas Day, 2016

4 Vampires, at Highgate Cemetery

5 Billionaires' Row; Salman Rushdie lived in a high-security house here for his own safety after Iran's Ayatollah Khomeini sentenced him to death for writing *The Satanic Verses*

6 Highwayman Dick Turpin; The Spaniards Inn

7 Arthur Winnington-Ingram, Bishop of London from 1901 to 1939, who owned much of the land in the area (and after whom The Bishop's Avenue is also named)

8 It was given to the nation by the Guinness family, founders of the Guinness Trust, providers of social housing; Kenwood House

9 Hampstead Garden Suburb; Labour Party; Harold Wilson, Peter Mandelson, grandson of Herbert Morrison

21.2

1 Either a cross or a crossroads, possibly a cross standing at a crossroads; Alexandra Palace

2 Dave Stewart; 145 Crouch Hill, where Stewart had recording studios

3 Boris Johnson

4 Theatre specialist, Frank Matcham

5 The Haringey Ladder

6 The Model Traffic Area – miniature roads with junctions, and signs, opened by the Department of Transport to teach children about road safety

7 Rookwood Road; Agapemonites

8 Murder Mile

9 Springfield Park; The White Lodge

21.3

1 The English Folk Dance and Song Society

2 The Popish Plot; Titus Oates

3 Alan Bennett; *The Lady in the Van*, Maggie Smith played Miss Mary Shepherd

4 Eton College; Hampstead Theatre (on Eton Avenue)

5 Kilburn Priory; Watling Street and the Kilburn (part of the Westbourne)

6 It was demolished by developers without planning permission; Westminster Council ordered it to be rebuilt brick by brick

7 Willesden; *White Teeth*

8 Primrose Hill; William Blake; 'For Tomorrow'

9 Primrose Hill; 'Jerusalem'

10 Swiss Cottage; Ye Olde Swiss Cottage

21.4

1 Race riots, which led to the first Notting Hill Carnival

2 Trellick Tower; Erno Goldfinger

3 Portobello Road; War of Jenkins' Ear; antiques market

4 Cemeteries; Isambard Kingdom Brunel is buried in Kensal Green Cemetery; Great Western Road is named after Brunel's Great Western Railway – and the railway itself runs along the side of Elkstone Road

5 Alan Coren; Giles Coren and Victoria Coren-Mitchell

6 Hendon FC

7 They are named after UK hill or mountain ranges; Golders Green Estate; Jean Simmons; *Guys and Dolls*, Sarah Brown

8 JG Ballard on the Westway

9 Kensington and Chelsea, Westminster, Hammersmith and Fulham, Brent, Barnet

21.5

1 Prince Albert (Queen Victoria's husband); Royal Albert Hall, Albert Memorial and Victoria & Albert Museum; it is named after the Hyde Park Great Exhibition of 1851, which Albert organised; Albertopolis

2 London Eye and The Shard

3 Bruce Springsteen, because he had overrun the curfew imposed by Westminster Council to placate residents in nearby Bayswater

4 The Prince Regent, future George IV; his mansion was Carlton House, as in Carlton House Terrace; John Nash; Marylebone Park

5 *Withnail and I*; *Hamlet*; they are in the wolves' enclosure in London Zoo, which is located in Regent's Park

6 It shares its name with a game – via the nearby London Underground station – on the long-running comedy series *I'm Sorry I Haven't a Clue*; Mornington Crescent

7 Sid Vicious

8 Seven elm trees

9 Arsenal, who originally played at Woolwich (home of the Royal Arsenal); the 'library', on account of the supposed lack of atmosphere

10 It is where Richard Whittington, future Mayor of London, is supposed to have stopped and turned back; the arched bridge that takes Hornsey Lane over Archway Road

21.6

1 Jimmy Page and Robbie Williams

2 Lime Grove Studios; Shepherd's Bush Empire; Wood Lane

3 Queen's Park Rangers; Loftus Road; White City Stadium; 1908, it was originally the stadium for the London Olympics of that year

4 Charing Cross Hospital; it was originally sited just off Strand in Charing Cross, but relocated to Hammersmith in 1973; further north in Du Cane Road, White City

5 The Dove has the world's smallest bar, but is still a popular spot for watching the Oxford and Cambridge Boat Race pass by; Oldfield swam into the river to stop the race as a declared protest against elitism

6 William Morris; electric telegraph

7 London Pride beer; Fuller's Brewery

8 Addison Road (after Joseph Addison); Holland House (in Holland Park)

9 Westfield shopping centre

21.7

1 Paddenswick House; Ravenscourt is a pun on his surname which derives from *corbeau*, French for 'raven'

2 Barn Elms Waterworks was converted into the London Wetland Centre; Wildfowl & Wetlands Trust, WWF's panda logo; Antarctic explorer Robert Falcon Scott

3 The River Café; Richard Rogers, who is married to chef and owner Ruth Rogers

4 The Cottagers; Craven Cottage was the name of a country house here; Stevenage Road

5 The Bishop of London; trees

6 The Hurlingham Club was the site of the first croquet match

7 A church

8 Thomas Cromwell, *Wolf Hall* (by Hilary Mantel)

9 Benjamin Disraeli (Disraeli Road)

10 The Putney Debates; Oliver Cromwell, a descendant of Thomas Cromwell, chaired the debates

21.8

1 Church Road; The All England Lawn Tennis and Croquet Club

2 Mosque (Fazl Mosque); Gressenhall Road

3 Thomas Hardy, who oversaw the removal of headstones in St Pancras Churchyard for the building of the East Midlands Railway and directed many of them to be placed around a tree which has grown into them, known now as the Hardy Tree; David Lloyd George

4 Wandsworth Common

5 The Clapham Junction rail crash, a passenger train collision that killed thirty-five people

6 The River Wandle; Wandle beer

7 Bolingbroke Grove (named after Henry St John, 1st Viscount Bolingbroke, who murdered a jury foreman, but was pardoned)

8 Emanuel School

9 Heathfield Road – they have both been inmates at Wandsworth Prison

21.9

1 Phyllis Pearsall, creator of the A–Z Map

2 Public art gallery; Dulwich Picture Gallery; tollgate

3 White picket fences

4 A walrus; it was stuffed from a hide and the taxidermist had never seen a real walrus so had to guess what one would look like; from tea (Horniman's Tea)

5 Elizabeth I

6 Tulse Hill; '24 Minutes from Tulse Hill' (Carter USM) and '24 Hours from Tulsa' (Gene Pitney)

7 Belair Park; River Effra

8 Dulwich College; Edward Alleyn; both went to school here; Bob Monkhouse, who also attended the school, was the only one of the three to be expelled

9 They are all part of the South Circular Road

21.10

1 Ship's ropes, or cables, which were manufactured here

2 Music Hall; Methodist mission

3 London Bridge Hospital stands on the site of St Olave's Church, named after St Olaf – King Olaf II of Norway. 'Tooley' is a corruption of St Olave

4 Northern Line and Jubilee Line; the Jubilee Line was renamed to celebrate Queen Elizabeth II's Silver Jubilee; Fleet Line (after the River Fleet)

5 Cinema; a workhouse; Charlie Chaplin

6 Horns Tavern; Surrey County Cricket Club was founded here; the Oval

7 Football; England and Scotland

8 Battle of Cable Street; Oswald Mosley's 'Blackshirts' and anti-fascist demonstrators

9 Shadwell

10 The Highway; Ratcliff Highway; Ratcliff Highway murders – two vicious multiple murders that took place in the area and were one of the era's most sensational crimes

11 The Shard; Renzo Piano

21.11

1 *Dixon of Dock Green*; East London Cemetery; he was the first person to be executed at the Tower of London in 167 years, for being a German spy

2 River Lea; Leyton

Before Harry Beck's first London Underground map was published in 1931, maps of the system had attempted to show the geographical location of the stations rather than their positions in relation to each other, but it was soon apparent that this made them very difficult to follow. Beck's solution quickly became a blueprint for others.

3 Shopping centre; Westfield Stratford City; Westfield London (Shepherd's Bush), the Metrocentre (Gateshead) and the Trafford Centre (Manchester)

4 Queen Elizabeth Olympic Park, opened for the London Olympics in 2012; West Ham United, London Stadium; Danny Boyle directed the 2012 Olympics opening ceremony in the stadium; West Ham previously played at Boleyn Ground in Upton Park

5 London Underground map

6 Leyton Orient FC; Brisbane Road; The O's

7 Abbey Road – the Beatles' more famous Abbey Road is in St John's Wood

8 London Aquatics Centre; Zaha Hadid

9 Maryland, named by a local landowner on returning from the US state, having made his money there

21.12

1 The crescent with the tightest curve; the London taxi is famous for its tight turning circle; Keystone Crescent; CCTV cameras

2 Hotel; rooms; The Royal National Hotel

3 Police force; Albert Finney played the title character in the 1963 film adaptation of the novel *Tom Jones*, written by Henry Fielding, who co-founded the Bow Street Runners

4 Inigo Jones; fruit and vegetables; Mister Punch (of Punch & Judy); London diarist Samuel Pepys

5 A menagerie of exotic animals (who were transferred to London Zoo)

6 The Savoy Hotel; traffic drives on the right; Claude Monet; he was head barman in the 1920s and 1930s, and author of *The Savoy Cocktail Book*

7 Methane gas burned off from the sewage system beneath it

8 Eleanor of Castile, wife of Edward I; urban legend claims that Elephant and Castle's name is a corruption of 'La Infanta de Castilla', which could have referred to Eleanor of Castile, but there is little evidence to support this theory

9 The old Euston Station's destruction spurred on the heritage movement that saved St Pancras Station from the same fate; John Betjeman

There are – or were – fourteen tributaries to the River Thames within the 9.6-km (6-mile) radius of Charing Cross that the Knowledge covers, from Bollo Brook in the west to the River Lea in the east. Ten of them are now below the surface.

➤➤ Suburbs

Suburbs.1

1 Terminal 2; Terminal 5
2 James Earl Ray; the assassination of Martin Luther King, Jr
3 Will Self; Stockwell
4 Eric Blair used the pen name George Orwell for the first time on the publication of *Down and Out in Paris and London*
5 Ossie Garvin
6 Art deco, Hoover
7 An eagle; it is the primary Polish national symbol
8 Princess Diana; Winston Churchill's
9 Ruislip; River Pinn, named after Pinner

Suburbs.2

1 McVitie's
2 Hindu temple (BAPS Shri Swaminarayan Mandir London)
3 *Private Eye* magazine publishes an occasional series of spoof logs from the fictional police station – and uses Neasden generally to represent suburbia
4 The crown of one of the old Wembley Stadium columns
5 Wembley Stadium staff; an iron tower similar to, but taller than, the Eiffel Tower in Paris
6 Harrow School; Harrow Road; they all contain part of either Edgware Road or Harrow Road
7 He was the first person to be killed by a passenger train; the first fatal road accident
8 Clement Attlee

Suburbs.3

1 Margaret Thatcher; Michael Portillo by Stephen Twigg, in Enfield Southgate
2 It's from the Old English for a meadow in which there are finches
3 Whetstone & Totteridge
4 Battle of Barnet, a critical battle in the Wars of the Roses; (Dr) David Livingstone
5 Barnet, from the Old English for 'land cleared by burning'

6 Barnet Fair – the cockney rhyming slang for hair is 'Barnet', from Barnet Fair
7 The Barnet branch of the Northern Line terminates at High Barnet and the Piccadilly Line terminates at Cockfosters
8 Enfield Chase

Suburbs.4

1 E17, which gave local band East 17 their name; they had a Christmas No 1 in 1994 with 'Stay Another Day'
2 William Morris's; Walthamstow Assembly Hall
3 Film studios
4 A pub, called the Crooked Billet
5 c. 800 years; the Kray twins
6 Queen Elizabeth I; Henry VIII; Epping Forest
7 A monument on Pole Hill marks true north from the Royal Observatory in Greenwich
8 Walthamstow – its name comes from the Old English for a place where strangers are welcome

Suburbs.5

1 Tate & Lyle's refinery overlooks it
2 Vietnam, in Stanley Kubrick's *Full Metal Jacket*; Beck was the gas works company's chairman
3 Sewage treatment plant
4 SS *Princess Alice*; many of the victims were poisoned by the untreated sewage in the water, a significant contributing factor in the creation of the sewage treatment plant
5 Housing estate; to create 'homes for heroes' – veterans of the First World War; George V and Queen Mary
6 Ford Motor Company
7 To transport pilgrims on their journey to Canterbury Cathedral
8 The A282 - the M25 is not a complete ring and reverts to an A road at the Dartford Crossing
9 A carving of the head of a horned bull (hence Hornchurch)

Suburbs.6

1 The Valley is the home ground of Charlton Athletic FC, nicknamed the Red Robins

2 Woolwich Arsenal; Thames Barrier flood defence and the free Woolwich Ferry

3 The UK's first building society (the Woolwich) and the UK's first McDonald's restaurant

4 *A Clockwork Orange*, directed by Stanley Kubrick; they have both served sentences at HMP Belmarsh, located at Thamesmead

5 The 1960s; it was ancient marshland and a military training ground

6 Pier; Denis Thatcher was chairman of chemical manufacturing firm Atlas, based in Erith, when he met his future wife (and future prime minister) Margaret Roberts

7 Mick Jagger

8 Trad jazz; George Melly

9 Linda Smith; Erith

Suburbs.7

1 The Richardsons; Ronnie Kray shot Richardson associate George Cornell in the Blind Beggar pub, Whitechapel

2 Eltham Palace; the art deco restoration was carried out by Stephen Courtauld, younger brother of Samuel, whose collection founded the gallery

3 David Bowie grew up in Plaistow Grove, lived in Haddon Hall (demolished in the 1980s, it stood where Shannon Way is now) with his first wife Angie, and played a free gig at the bandstand in 1969

4 Chislehurst Caves

5 Archbishop of Canterbury

6 Bernie Ecclestone

7 Croydon

Suburbs.8

1 The Priory, a private psychiatric hospital well known as an addiction treatment centre, often attended by celebrities in 'rehab'; Marc Bolan, killed in a car crash at this spot

2 St Paul's Cathedral

3 Photography – he specialised in pictures of humans and animals in movement and his images showed that when a horse runs, all four of its legs leave the ground at the same time; artist Francis Bacon

4 Cardinal Wolsey; George II; real tennis

5 Dwight D Eisenhower; 'Chestnut Sunday', when droves of Londoners come to admire the blossoming avenue of horse chestnut trees in the park; Sir Christopher Wren oversaw the planting of the trees

6 Royal Parks; Richmond Park and Bushy Park; Green Park, Greenwich Park, Hyde Park, Kensington Gardens, Regent's Park and St James's Park

7 Wimbledon Common; both are names of Wombles: (Uncle) Bulgaria and Tobermory

8 Fenton the dog, chasing deer in Richmond Park

Suburbs.9

1 Richard Boyle, Earl of Burlington; artist William Hogarth

2 Captain James Cook; it is the world's oldest pot plant; UNESCO World Heritage Sites: Greenwich, Tower of London, Westminster

3 The National Archives

4 Twickenham Studios, where the Beatles made their films *A Hard Day's Night* (1964) and *Help!* (1965)

5 Eel Pie Island; Strawberry Hill Gothic, Strawberry Hill House; Horace Walpole

6 He was televised sport's first streaker

7 The furthest inland point of the tidal River Thames (Teddington Lock)

8 Feltham Young Offenders Institute, just west of Hanworth; in 2002 Armitage made Bafta-winning musical documentary *Feltham Sings* at the institute, featuring some of the inmates here

Index

Credits

. . . .

About the author

Hailing from Holmfirth, West Yorkshire, Ian studied English at the University of Leeds, graduating in 2000. After a variety of jobs including pizza delivery driver, restaurant pianist, nightclub reviewer and baker's assistant he set about learning the Knowledge in 2008 while working as an administrator at the *Guardian*. Ian received his Green Badge – the All London taxi driver's licence – in 2012, after more than four years of intensive study. Now a licensed London taxi driver, he also contributes to the *Guardian*, writes a blog called Words on the Street, and performs regularly as lead singer, pianist and songwriter with London-based band Ian Beetlestone & the Drowning Rats. Ian lives in Islington with his cat, Larry.

Author acknowledgements

I might like to think I've done comparatively well in picking up knowledge (with a small 'k') of London in the miles I've clocked up since moving to the city in 2005, starting the Knowledge in 2008 and driving a cab since 2012. But I've picked up a comparatively large trove of London books in that time, too. Many of those – along with countless websites and trips down search engine rabbit holes – have been essential aids in coming up with the questions in this book. Especially useful have been A.D. Mills' *A Dictionary of London Place Names*, Derek Sumeray and John Sheppard's *London Plaques*, Leigh Hatts' *London's 100 Best Churches*, Ed Glinert's brilliant *The London Compendium*, and Ben Weinreb, Christopher Hibbert, Julia Keay and John Keay's *The London Encyclopaedia*. The wonderful and idiosyncratic *Nairn's London*, by Ian Nairn, has already been mentioned, as, of course, has the indispensable *London A–Z*. The Knowledge (large 'K') of London, meanwhile, I learned with the inestimable guidance and support of Dean Warrington, his colleagues, and my fellow students – now fellow cabbies – at the Wizann Knowledge School in East London.

Publisher acknowledgements

Special thanks to David Stephens, Louisa Keyworth and Neill Donaldson at Lovell Johns for all their help and assistance in supplying the maps in the book.

Illustrations by Dave Jones, with the following acknowledgements: 'Taxi' icon by Chazz Basuta; 'Brompton Oratory' icon by Louis 4130 (p.27), 'Dartboard' icon by Graphic Tigers (p.53), 'Royal Crown' icon by Vectors Market (pp.75, 169) all from thenounproject.com.